THE NAVY AND THE NATION

THE NAVY AND THE NATION

AUSTRALIA'S MARITIME POWER IN THE 21ST CENTURY

VICE ADMIRAL TIM BARRETT

MELBOURNE UNIVERSITY PRESS

MELBOURNE UNIVERSITY PRESS
An imprint of Melbourne University Publishing Limited
Level 1, 715 Swanston Street, Carlton, Victoria 3053, Australia
mup-info@unimelb.edu.au
www.mup.com.au

First published 2017
Text © Commonwealth of Australia, 2017
Design and typography © Melbourne University Publishing Limited, 2017

Cover design by Philip Campbell Design
Typeset by Sonya Murphy, Typeskill
Printed in Australia by McPherson's Printing Group

National Library of Australia Cataloguing-in-Publication entry

Barrett, Tim, author.

The navy and the nation: Australia's maritime power in the twenty-first century/Vice
Admiral Tim Barrett AO, CSC, RAN, Chief of Navy.

9780522871586 (paperback)
9780522871593 (ebook)

Includes index.

Australia. Royal Australian Navy.
    Australia. Royal Australian Navy—History—21st century.
    Sea-power—Australia—21st century.
    Naval strategy—Australia—21st century.
    National security—Australia—21st century.
    Australia—History, Naval—21st century.

CONTENTS

THE SHAPE OF THINGS TO COME

MOST PEOPLE THINK that Navy is something else. They know it exists, they may even have a rough idea of what it is for, but they don't think it's got much to do with them. They're wrong. The Navy is a national enterprise in which everyone is involved and which delivers peace and security to everyone in the country.

This enterprise is a two-way street, and must be a two-way street.

Going one way, the Navy offers peace and security. Going the other, the people offer support and contribution. Only when the street is a properly mutual two-way exchange between the Navy and the citizens can this bargain, this contract, deliver what it needs to.

I must admit, not all sailors fully realise this, or what it really means either. For me, the significance and implication of the bond between the Navy and the nation really hit home when I was given the unexpected and singular honour of appointment as Chief of the Service.

Napoleon's famous observation that all Service personnel carry a Marshal's baton in their kitbag might have been an encouragement to performance and endurance for the conscripts in the first of the world's mass armies. The fact is, however, that most of us do not even think about it.

So it was for me: promotion to Chief of the Royal Australian Navy (RAN) in 2014 was unanticipated.

The first thing one does as Chief of Service is to begin thinking of the responsibilities that go with the job and how one is going to meet them. There were, of course, the examples of the excellent leaders of the past, going back to Vice Admirals Stevenson and Synnot—the professional heads of the Navy in the year that I joined. Before them, the list of distinguished naval officers goes back to Rear Admiral Creswell, the inaugural director of the Commonwealth Naval Forces. There were also the examples of the leaders of the Army and the Air Force, as well as the Chiefs of the Defence Force—people of enormous ability, dedication and strength of character.

All the wise words of advice one receives from one's predecessors notwithstanding, there is no option but to work it out for oneself.

It is perhaps a commonplace to say that one grows into the job—but it is no less true for that. Many factors combine to distinguish the present-day job from that of one's predecessors: the fast-moving world in which we live; the challenges facing governments as they grapple with the fluidity of political, economic and social circumstances; the operational tempo of the Australian Defence Force itself; the demands on each of the Services as they recruit and train their people and maintain their capabilities; the pressure to stimulate renewal while maintaining standards and values. These, and more, characterise the environment in which military leaders must ultimately define themselves.

Over the past two decades, the command structures of the Australian Defence Force have evolved. Following the July 2016 amendment of the *Defence Act* (1903), the Chief of the Defence Force (CDF) now has unambiguous command of the Defence Force. The Vice Chief of the Defence Force assists the CDF. The Chiefs of the three Services 'command' their Services as they exercise day-to-day control and responsibility for all their personnel, and for materiel like ships and establishments, as they prepare for joint operations. The Service Chiefs are also responsible for capability development, for making sure that their Services are positioned for future operations. The Service Chiefs assign forces to the Chief of Joint Operations (CJOPS), for operations, whether in combat such as Afghanistan and the

Middle East, or conducting humanitarian operations, or engaged in international exercises.

The key responsibility of the Service Chiefs is to manage the capabilities of their respective Services—to develop and lead their people, and to maintain the systems, capabilities and platforms that provide the backbone of their combat forces.

For Chiefs of Navy, one of the key responsibilities is to ensure that the Navy has the forces that the CDF might need to call upon to assign to the CJOPS for operations. So it is their job to manage the Navy's people together with the ships, submarines and aircraft in a way that provides government with all the options it needs to deploy the Defence Force to meet the nation's security interests. This is a job that all Chiefs of Service take very seriously, since ultimately the lives and welfare of their people depend on the integrity and capacity of the systems they operate.

Apart from the responsibilities that go with the job of Chief of Service, one quickly comes to recognise that there are leadership demands that impact directly on the people one is privileged to lead. In this sense, leadership needs to be both transactional—managing the day-to-day issues—and transformational—managing for the future and for the unknown. Leadership is not just about our Service personnel's welfare and training, important as that is. It extends to their personal and professional development, especially when change is accelerating and the attendant uncertainties and insecurities need to be managed.

When he published *The Shape of Things to Come* in 1933, H.G.Wells imagined a kind of parallel universe with an alternative history. He might have saved himself the effort. The second half of the twentieth century, with all its twists and turns, was as unimaginable in the inter-war years as the twenty-first century is now. The only certainty is change. Thus, the Navy's prospects are set out in *Plan Pelorus*, a plan that recognises our strategic future will be marked with the discontinuities and ambiguities that have always confronted leaders. What the transformational leader needs to do is to ensure that the strategies and operational concepts that underpin present and future planning are able to deal with uncertainty and unpredictability, discontinuity and ambiguity.

An increasingly important demand on leaders, irrespective of the enterprise for which they might happen to exercise responsibility, is to provide clear direction and guidance, not only for the task at hand but also for the tasks that might be down the track. For Chiefs of Navy, this means a constant effort to communicate, develop, explain and encourage so that the Navy's people are able to deal confidently and effectively with both present and future challenges. This is no small matter: the ability to deal with present and future challenges requires agility of mind and flexibility of temperament that depends on having clear goals, sound operating principles and the strength of mind and character to deal with the unforeseen. These qualities go to the very core of a modern, adaptable and successful navy.

The RAN is on the cusp of major reinvestment, and the institutional and organisational changes that will inevitably follow in consequence. The Defence White Paper issued in February 2016 charts a new course for the Navy as it re-equips itself with new offshore patrol boats, a new class of frigate, a new and expanded submarine force, and continues the acquisition of the new *Hobart* class Air Warfare Destroyer. So, the question is: how does the Navy prepare for the shape of things to come?

Frankly, renewal on this scale is daunting. Its management demands clarity of purpose, effective communication to ensure that everyone knows what the task is and what they are expected to do, and leadership at all levels that encourages, empowers and rewards. We need to think differently. In other words, by reviewing our basic operating concepts, reimagining the way that Navy should view itself in the twenty-first century, re-examining our assumptions and, most importantly, re-engineering our *modus operandi*—especially the way we manage domestic and international relationships—and our professional behaviours, Navy will be better positioned to take advantage of the promise of things to come. As our friends in the Army are wont to say, 'time spent on reconnaissance is seldom wasted'.[1]

So it is for this reason that it is essential to set out a clear approach to this task in an easily digestible form to ensure that the Navy's leaders at all levels, together with the dedicated and hard-working people who constitute the Navy's many teams, understand what the Navy is, what it is for, and how it might go about implementing the new demands and opportunities that government has generated. Hence this essay is called *The Navy and the*

Nation. This title has been used before: by David Stevens and John Reeve in their fine collection of essays a decade ago (just as they were beaten to the punch over a century earlier, as we shall see at the end of this essay).[2] Their purpose, however, was to track the influence of the Navy on modern Australia. The intention of this essay is less to track the influence of the Navy on the nation than it is to understand how the Navy fits with the nation. It provides a background that will help everyone in the Navy to appreciate why it is that government has decided to make such large and continuing investments in our national naval capabilities, and to provide the public at large with some of the conceptual thinking that underpins the Navy as it goes about meeting the strategic and operational challenges of the twenty-first century.

What this essay attempts to do, in a relatively extended form, is to provide a coherent context within which the various ideas can be linked to provide a conceptual overview—a 'narrative' as contemporary commentators like to demand.

The Navy, of course, has no truly separate existence apart from the community in which it is embedded and which sustains it. The Australian people support us, and the taxpayer funds us. As the eminent British strategic analyst Geoffrey Till has pointed out, 'the forces engaged in maritime operations … are expensive, hard to replace and even the smallest units represent a sizeable investment in human resources whose loss can be sudden and instantaneous and very hard for governments and publics to bear'.[3]

Consequently, the wider Australian public would doubtless be interested in finding out how the Navy sees itself, and how it intends to deliver and employ the capabilities that government has mandated for it. As this essay will argue, the Navy is a national enterprise. It is deeply embedded in the nation. To meet the challenges before it, the Navy has to take advantage of capabilities the nation offers and, equally, the nation must be able to leverage the capabilities of the Navy. This demands habits of reformation and transformation that go beyond what we have had to do in the past. Again, we must think differently.

We need to appreciate the power and opportunities that disruptive technologies will create for us. We have to understand that Navy needs new ways of managing its relationships with industry, with the investment community, with the nation's universities and technical colleges, with entrepreneurs and innovators, with allies and partners and, of course, with its fellow Services, the Army and the Air Force and the broader defence organisation.

Without trust and respect—both of them mutual qualities, dependent on the good will of both parties to a relationship—any effort to recreate the Navy as a national enterprise will fail. For Navy's part, an inability to understand that industry must generate profits if it is both to survive and to be able to deliver future capabilities will destroy the very thing that we are trying to create—national resilience based on a strong and innovative industrial and technological economy. And for industry, the inability to partner and to share risk, or to mistakenly see Navy as a purse to be plundered, will only guarantee failure.

But old habits die hard. Government, through the White Paper 2016, and through agreement of the 2015 *First Principles Review*, has given us the chance to redesign the way that we do business in delivering the defence capabilities the nation needs. It is up to us to grasp the opportunity.

In the wider community of interest for which this essay is also intended, the manufacturing, industrial, technological and investment sectors are at front of mind. Not only should the leaders of these sectors read and understand how the Navy might position itself for these new opportunities, but they should also begin to join the conversation that is a necessary part of realising these opportunities. Industry leaders should embark upon a conversation with the leaders of the Navy in the same way that naval leaders should talk to them.

Innovation comes from surprising places, and is always the result of the 'aha!' moment that rewards sustained inquiry. It is not limited to the owners or users of systems, but so often derives from the designers and constructors who build them. For that reason, the Navy needs to benefit from the feedback loops that will be a necessary part of a new way of doing business. We all talk, often loudly, when things go wrong. We need to talk when things are going right, well before things derail. This is what is meant by the 'conversation' that we need to sustain.

Most of the leaders of our key national institutions are acutely aware that our society is changing as it learns to adjust to demographic pressures, the evolving expectations of our fellow citizens, the fluidity and variability in the career choices available to young people, the pressures of managing family and professional demands, the remarkable and timely expansion in the role that women play in our national enterprise—to name just a few factors driving change. Just as the Navy will be affected by the pace of change, so it needs to participate in managing change and benefiting from it. Inevitably, the naval career of the twenty-first century will differ significantly from that of the twentieth century. We need to prepare for change, in order to make the most of it.

Finally, the up-and-coming cohort of young naval leaders should develop a sense of excitement and enthusiasm for what is to come. Our young sailors and young officers at the beginning of their careers will continue to expand their horizons, regarding their life in the Navy not just as a career but as a contribution to the marvellous enterprise Australia has become. Their ability to communicate, with authority and conviction, what the Navy is and does will be central to their ability to manage and leverage the complex professional and personal relationships that will mark their passage to seniority and leadership. And if this essay helps them to achieve that, then it will have realised the hope that has underpinned the writing of it.

This essay is not to place the Navy above or beyond the other Services. Recognising the principles of 'One Defence,' which were articulated in the *First Principles Review*, this essay seeks to explain the contribution the Navy makes to the whole of Australian defence, and to the whole of the Australian nation.

THE RAN'S HERITAGE

H.G. WELLS IS NOT the only writer to have created a book title that came into common parlance: 'the shape of things to come' is often used to denote a deliberate plan for the future, overlooking the novel's description of a future society characterised by misery, oppression and disease. So, too, the title of Donald Horne's iconic critique of Australian complacency, *The Lucky Country*, is often repeated without the irony that characterised Horne's use of the phrase.[4]

Yet one can understand why a less self-critical and perhaps more self-absorbed generation might come to see itself as 'lucky'. It is. And central to Australia's good fortune, at least so far as our national institutions are concerned, is the fact that we have inherited the traditions of Westminster and the legacy of British political, economic and military institutions as they evolved over the eight centuries since *Magna Carta*.

At the time of Federation, the colonial navies—which, though lacking capability, were accurate cultural copies of the Royal Navy (RN)—coalesced to form the Commonwealth Naval Forces.[5] In this historical sense, the RAN grew out of the RN, with its long tradition of professionalism, its focus on seamanship, its subordination to the elected government, its respect for the law and its reputation for courage. Indeed, as David Cannadine has written, to be Australian and to be British was the same thing.[6]

The first four governors of the nascent colony were naval officers. The fourth, William Bligh RN, generated considerable controversy as an administrator, though there was no doubt about his seamanship. Eventually promoted to Vice Admiral of the Blue, Bligh put in place the administrative and management structures that enabled his successor, Lachlan Macquarie—subsequently promoted to Major General—to set colonial New South Wales on its feet.

From the arrival of the First Fleet in 1788, the RN provided the naval defence of the settlement in Sydney Cove and its principal communication with the outside world, especially London. In 1859, Sydney became the principal base of a separate British naval station and, until the outbreak of World War I, the RN maintained a squadron in Australian waters.[7] As a growing number of Australians took on responsibility for manning and leading a progressively more Australian naval presence, so young Australians went to Britain for their training; a practice that continued until well into the second half of the twentieth century. Exchange arrangements continue today.

Our two navies have also enjoyed close links at both the family and personal level. My father was a RN officer, and I was christened onboard HMS *Victorious*. We continue to maintain the longstanding practice of seconding officers between our navies and, like many of my colleagues, I have served in British warships. Just as the RN is in the RAN's DNA, so too is the Westminster system in our governmental DNA.

Australia's early administrators established British constitutional and legal practice as the Australian way of doing business. For governments, the defence of the people and the land they occupy, together with provision of the physical, economic and social security of the citizens, are the central planks that support legitimacy, credibility and authority. They are also at the heart of the contract between the people and their government.

We in Australia have not just been lucky—we have been blessed. Since Federation, governments have honoured this contract, with varying degrees of success it must be said, as they have balanced the myriad fiscal, social and political pressures that characterise modern democracies. The Great

Depression, for instance, which had such a terrible impact on the lives of so many Australians, led to an under-investment in national defence capacity in the years immediately before World War II.

But the same cannot be said of the years leading up to World War I, as the newly formed Commonwealth governments grappled with political volatility, the challenges of integrating federal administrative systems, and the monumental task of creating a national identity.

If Rear Admiral William Creswell was the father of the Royal Australian Navy, Alfred Deakin, our second Prime Minister, was its principal architect. For it was Deakin who gave early expression to the political philosophy that continues to provide the fundamental *raison d'être* of the national defence enterprise today.

Defence, said Deakin, is the ultimate guardian of liberty, the freedom— grounded in the rule of law—that flows from the recognition that each citizen has dignity and value. And, in Deakin's view, any attack on that dignity and value is an attack on the nation as a whole. Deakin's articulation of the policy underpinnings of the national defence enterprise rings as true today as it did in 1907. It is worth quoting at length what he had to say in the House of Representatives on Friday 13 December 1907:

> If we lost the whole of our financial possessions we should miss them much less than if we were robbed of liberty, constitutional freedom, civilization, and social status.
>
> One hesitates even to consider such prospects, and yet one must recollect that there are grave contingencies to be kept in view, if it be only at the back of our minds.
>
> None of us can conceive Australians in serfdom. Or subject to an alien rule.
>
> Although the incredible consequences that would follow from the obliteration of our race and nationality cannot be compassed by the imagination, we can never forget that what we have most to defend first and last is our national life and ideals more precious than life of the breathing frame …
>
> What we seek is not the development of what is sometimes termed a military as distinguished from a martial spirit.

What we aim at is the maximum of good citizenship, with the spirit of patriotism as the chief motive power of a civic defence force.

For always, behind the weapons, behind the organization, behind the gun, there is the man. It is in the character and capacity of its manhood that the real strength and energy of resistance of a people must be found …

Despite the anachronistic language, there is no challenging the importance of Deakin's words: the moral purpose of the people is the rock on which national defence stands.

As he continued his speech to the Parliament on that Friday in 1907, he outlined his vision for the RAN. It is a vision that continues to inspire our modern Navy:

In this country we accept the minimum of professional militarism strictly so-called, and in considering our national policy generally we require a maximum of navalism, if I may coin such a word.

After all, the British Empire itself and all its parts depend for their unity and guarantee of freedom upon the Navy.

That is its first line of defence, and we in Australia are distinguished in this particular, because we must rely more upon it than any other part of the Empire.

Ours is an island continent, and its best defence will be that which prevents an invader from ever setting his foot upon our shores.[8]

Deakin was, of course, providing a contemporary answer to that age-old question: 'Is there anything for which a nation has the right to spill the blood of its children?'

But the thing that does justify the expenditure of blood and treasure in our democratic society is any attempt to constrain the personal liberty of our citizens, because that is what defines us as citizens. Deakin got it. He also understood implicitly that there is a community of values.

While, in 1907, that community, from an Australian perspective, was the British Empire, in present-day terms it is the community of democratic nations that place the individual liberty of their citizens at the centre of their political values. This is what drove the overwhelming support of democratic nations for the US as it confronted the horror of 9/11, and what inspired Prime Minister John Howard to invoke the ANZUS treaty in support of the US for the first time in the treaty's history.

The centrality of values in determining the entire *raison d'être* of a modern democracy was nowhere better set out than in President Franklin D. Roosevelt's State of the Union address to the US Congress in 1941. With both poignancy and prescience, he enumerated the four fundamental freedoms without which there can be no democracy:

> The first is freedom of speech and expression—everywhere in the world.
>
> The second is freedom of every person to worship God in his own way—everywhere in the world.
>
> The third is freedom from want—which, translated into world terms, means economic understandings which will secure to every nation a healthy peacetime life for its inhabitants—everywhere in the world.
>
> The fourth is freedom from fear—which, translated into world terms, means a world-wide reduction of armaments to such a point and in such a thorough fashion that no nation will be in a position to commit an act of physical aggression against any neighbor—anywhere in the world.
>
> That is no vision of a distant millennium. It is a definite basis for a kind of world attainable in our own time and generation. That kind of world is the very antithesis of the so-called new order of tyranny which the dictators seek to create with the crash of a bomb.[9]

When one recalls that this address was delivered just eleven months before the bombing of Pearl Harbor, Roosevelt's speech can be seen as a call to arms that would see the US shoulder the greater part of the burden in the fight against fascism on two fronts, Europe and the Pacific.

Australia's national conversation tends to be conducted in less lofty terms: we are more inclined to give public expression to our national values in the simple but elegant term 'rule of law'. In 2002, the Australian Chief of the Defence Force, Admiral Chris Barrie, issued a publication titled *The Australian Approach to Warfare*. It says, among other things:

The Australian Defence Force is an important national institution in Australia. Its core function is to defend Australia from armed attack. In carrying out this and all its other functions, the Australian Defence Force is dependent on the support of the Australian people, is governed by the rule of law, and is subject to the direction of the Commonwealth Government as the civil authority.[10]

The US Chairman of the Joint Chiefs or the UK Chief of the Defence Staff could just as well have said this. An attack on any country upholding these principles is an attack on all countries that uphold these principles. This principle is what drove the nations of the free world to coalesce around the fight against tyranny in World War I and in World War II, and what continues to inspire the 'coalition of the willing' to work jointly to defeat those who would advocate terrorism as a means of global oppression.

Values are what we defend

War is always the continuation of policy by other means, as the great German strategic thinker Carl von Clausewitz put it. In wars of aggression, the policy in question, of course, is the policy of domination, the policy of the expansion of national power, the policy of the enslavement of other peoples and the policy of expropriation of their national treasure. And the means to achieve that is armed force.

And in wars of self-defence, the policy in question is the well-being of the citizens, their freedom, their way of life, their prosperity and their ability to function as a community free from oppression. Clausewitz argued that defence is the stronger form of war. He wrote: 'We have already stated what defence is—simply the more effective form of war: a means to win a victory that enables one to take the offensive after superiority has been gained; that is, to proceed to the active object of the war'.[11] His argument is that, when a nation is under attack, it has the united political, moral, emotional and economic strength of the citizens to act to protect the freedom of the people. And as the history of war in the twentieth century demonstrated, Clausewitz was, for the most part, quite right.

But his argument has an interesting consequence: because defence is the stronger form of war, it must remain at the forefront of national policy if it is to provide the constant reassurance that democratic peoples demand if they are to go about their ordinary occupations and build both national strength and national resilience.

While we might all search for constancy, order and predictability, the fact is that there is an intrinsic randomness at play in world affairs. There is a constant ambiguity in global political affairs, and discontinuity and unpredictability characterise the strategic environment in which governments create their defence policies.

Most of us prefer simplicity and clarity. Yet the curious fact is that ambiguity and discontinuity actually provide us with critically important opportunities that go to the heart of strategic policy-making. War is a fundamentally human activity: people make war. So those of us who understand the inherent strength of a defensive strategy also understand that our antagonists also prefer simplicity and clarity. And that is where they are most vulnerable, because we exploit that preference by maximising their uncertainty. We do that by leveraging ambiguity and discontinuity for our own strategic ends.

In short, our aim is to mess with the minds of our adversaries.

NAVAL POWER, MARITIME POWER AND STRATEGIC REACH

T HE INTRINSIC VALUE of the person and the freedoms that flow from that basic concept have provided the core *raison d'être* for our national defence effort since Federation. It has also provided the fundamental rationale for the Navy throughout our 115-year history. To understand where we are going, it is important to understand where we have come from. It is even more important to understand the dynamics that have underpinned that evolution as the relationship between naval power and strategic maritime power has continued to evolve.

To put the issue in another way: if we do not grasp the fundamental taxonomy of our national defence systems, and, in this case, the organisation and coordination of the systems that have enabled Navy's continuous development for over a century, we cannot hope to develop the systems on which we will deliver the security outcomes mandated by government in the decades ahead.

As we look back to the ANZAC landings—the biggest amphibious landings of World War I—it is important to recognise the crucial role played by the RN and the RAN in the Dardanelles Campaign. That campaign required tactical and operational innovation of a kind and on a scale not seen previously. New forms of naval power—submarines and the prototype aircraft carrier—were tactical innovations with enduring strategic effect. As the Australian submarine *AE2* was running amok in the Sea of Marmora, exposing the Turkish Navy to a new form of warfare, HMS *Ark Royal* provided the aerial surveillance and terrain mapping that enabled both effective naval gunfire support and ground operations. The significance of *Ark Royal* will return a little later in this essay.

But the evolution of naval power in the twentieth century went far beyond the development of battleships and heavy cruisers, the ability to mount complex amphibious operations, or to mount submarine operations on the scale of the imperial German *Kriegsmarine* under Grand Admiral von Tirpitz—a significant strategic innovator in his own right, and a person deeply influenced by the writings of Alfred Thayer Mahan, the US maritime strategist whom we shall meet a little further on in this essay. In essence, between the Battle of Jutland and the Battle of the Coral Sea, naval power evolved into maritime power. So we need to look briefly at the Battles of Jutland, the Atlantic and the Coral Sea to trace this evolution in reasonably accessible terms.

The Battle of Jutland

While some naval historians have described the Battle of Jutland as 'indecisive' or 'a stalemate', it was undoubtedly a strategic success for Britain and the RN. Scheer's High Seas Fleet withdrew, and was not seen again for the duration of the war. As a contemporary American columnist summed it up, 'The German fleet has assaulted her British jailer but remains in prison'.[12]

Jutland was the first encounter of fleets that looked even vaguely modern, and a battle of unimaginable intensity. It remains one of the costliest battles ever fought.[13] Jutland was also the last set engagement between battle fleets, depending, of course, on your definition of battle fleets. As the RN's losses suggest, mass at sea was not the determinant. The costs imposed on the High Seas Fleet were simply unacceptable from a strategic perspective. The German fleet lost its capacity for strategic manoeuvre. It went home, and stayed there.[14]

Andrew Gordon, author of *The Rules of the Game: Jutland and British Naval Command*, among the most penetrating analyses of the Battle of

Jutland, concludes his study with a set of twenty-eight 'Blinding Glimpses of the Obvious'—the lessons learnt. They are all gems. But the one that any Chief of Navy, as the person responsible to government for preparing the Navy to serve the nation in time of war, would find the most disturbing is the twelfth 'BGO', in which Gordon observes, 'A service which neglects to foster a conceptual grasp of specialized subjects will have too few warriors able to interrogate the specialists'.[15] This comment is at once an indictment of the complacency that infected the RN in the comfortable decades before World War I and a challenge to modern-day naval leaders.

Self-doubt and the resultant self-examination are critical attributes of the warrior. An inherent skepticism and a constant questioning of doctrinal mantras are the essential tools of strategic and operational relevance. Similarly, the Navy assures seaworthiness only by the deep and unceasing questioning of fundamentals.

Warfare is always a contest of political will where the crucial weapon is the mind. The true test of leadership is agility of mind and efficiency in decision-making. Our capacity for strategic manoeuvre rests in our ability to ensure that our doctrine that gives effect to strategic intent is clear, up-to-date and properly understood by our fighting men and women. In this most fundamental sense, war at sea in World War I truly was 'the continuation of policy by other means'.[16] And that is what we must remember in present-day strategic circumstances. The contemporary significance of these ideas will be illuminated later in this essay.

The Battle of the Atlantic

The Battle of the Atlantic was the longest sea battle in history, bringing new dimensions to naval power, such as operations research and joint and combined sea and air operations, enabling the RN ultimately to break the U-boat threat, thereby achieving the strategic outcome of blockading Germany and maintaining supplies to Britain. The significance of the Battle of the Atlantic was not lost on Britain's wartime Prime Minister. As Churchill said in 1941, 'can you wonder that it is the Battle of the Atlantic which holds the first place in the thoughts of those upon whom rests responsibility for procuring the victory?'[17]

Initially, operational relations between the RN and the US Navy (USN) were pretty testy. US Fleet Admiral Ernest King's anglophobia and his apparent antipathy towards the RN imposed particular limitations on joint operations. The RN's preference for convoying merchant vessels rather than leaving them at the less-than-tender mercies of the German U-boats was not shared by its US counterpart.

But the mathematics of operations research demonstrated that, for any given number of ships, travelling in a single convoy rather than in smaller convoys optimised success. The RN also discovered that long-range maritime patrol aircraft, operating with destroyers and corvettes, could counter and defeat the U-boats. Like Jutland, it came at a tremendous cost, but its strategic outcome was undeniable.

The Battle of the Atlantic was the dominating factor all through the war in Western Europe. Not for one moment could Churchill and the Allied leaders forget that everything happening elsewhere, on land, at sea or in the air depended ultimately on its outcome. Maritime power is ultimately the key to success in war.

The Battle of the Coral Sea

In the Pacific, the Battle of the Coral Sea began the defeat of Japan. This was the first naval battle in history where the opposing fleets could not see each other, at sea level. Yet they inflicted massive damage on each other, with the early tactical advantage appearing to lie with Japan, in a way that was somewhat reminiscent of the Battle of Jutland. Yet the strategic advantage clearly lay with the Allies.

Because of the damage inflicted on two of the Japanese carriers (one was structurally damaged and the other lost many of its aircraft), the Battle of the Coral Sea (4–8 May 1942) set the scene for the allied naval victory at the Battle of Midway (4–7 June 1942), where the air assets of the opposing sides were more evenly matched. More importantly, the Battle of the Coral Sea was the necessary precursor of the Battle of Leyte Gulf (23–26 October 1944), perhaps the greatest naval battle in history. The defeat of the Imperial Japanese Navy was critical to MacArthur's recapture of the Philippines.

Of course, there was a basic difference between the war in Europe and the war in the Pacific. Whereas the European theatre was fundamentally a continental war, the Pacific theatre was fundamentally an archipelagic war. Without in any way detracting from the strategic and logistic brilliance of the amphibious landing in Normandy, the fact is that the US and Australia conducted over forty amphibious landings during the Pacific War, each one of them with its peculiar logistic and operational dynamics.

Our joint operations with the USN during the Pacific War set the scene for our consequent alliance with the US. But more than that, it hard-wired partnership and interdependence into our maritime DNA, a subject for later discussion in this essay. And for the first Australian Chief of the Naval Staff, Vice Admiral Sir John Collins, partnership straddled both the RN and the USN. As Captain of HMAS *Sydney*, he participated in the Battle of the Mediterranean in 1940, and was then commander of the combined Australian–US Task Force 74 in HMAS *Australia*. He was badly injured as a result of the first kamikaze attack in the Pacific War, when HMAS *Australia* was hit in the lead-up to the Battle of Leyte Gulf.

For both the UK and Australia, the trajectory of our respective learning curves between the end of World War I and the end of World War II was as transformative as it was steep. Our navies moved from a focus on platforms as the key components of our fleets to a concentration on the integration of capabilities to generate strategic naval systems.

And this is where we return to Gallipoli and HMS *Ark Royal*. Within just over four decades, naval power evolved into maritime power by incorporating both air power and submarines as intrinsic components of both force projection and fleet protection. And this period also saw interdependence and partnership emerge as the defining strategic advantage over adversaries that sought to constrain and curtail the freedoms that define our nations and our societies. Moreover, the emergence of a large number of enabling technologies, particularly signals intelligence, has delivered force multipliers that further reinforce this evolution, and promise continuing transformation.

THE NATURE OF CONTEMPORARY MARITIME POWER

THE WORLD HAS moved on inexorably since 1942. While the Battle of the Coral Sea brought into play a totally new dimension of maritime power—the air battle—it was, like HMS *Ark Royal's* deployment to ANZAC Cove, both innovative and experimental.

The Korean War, the Vietnam War, the Falklands War and the first Iraq War saw navies progressively more able to dominate the under-, on- and above-sea domains. Developments, especially in automation, missiles, weapons engineering, sensors, communications and stealth technologies, began to afford tactical and strategic options that Vice Admiral Fletcher of the USN and Rear Admiral Crace of the RAN could only have dreamt of in 1942 as they confronted the Imperial Japanese Navy.

But while the USN remains the dominant naval and maritime power, other navies are catching up. The Russian Navy remains a powerful and constantly modernising force. The Indian Navy is growing in both capability and reach. And the Chinese Navy has already demonstrated its ability to project power at long range. The Chinese Navy's deployment early in 2014 of an amphibious assault ship and two Air Warfare Destroyers, together with the deployment of a nuclear attack submarine (SSN) in 2015 into the Indian Ocean are palpable reminders of how ambition and reach are coming together in China.

As we reflect on our actions in the conduct of war, the blinding glimpse of the most obvious is that reality has the terrible habit of testing theory. While we continue to build on the doctrinal assumptions of the past, we must be vigilant in ensuring that they remain fit for purpose. The Battle of the Nile and the Battle of Trafalgar are glorious in the annals of the RN. But we would not for a moment contemplate resurrecting the doctrine[18] on which Nelson based his victories. So, before embarking on an analysis of what the Navy is in the contemporary context, why we need a navy and how it operates as a national enterprise, it is important that we identify a few of the conceptual building blocks and explain them. Like most organisations, the Navy has a few 'buzz-words', though they are pretty simply explained.

Sea power: Sea control and sea denial

If there is a core concept that has underpinned traditional consideration of sea power, it is the interlinked ideas of sea control and sea denial. 'Sea control' and 'sea denial' are important terms in the discussion of sea power, but for some people they are terms that have become mere mantras—concepts around which people rally but which have come to mean whatever they want them to mean, very convenient but totally inconclusive.

In his important book *Seapower*, Geoffrey Till identifies the complexity that has surrounded seapower concepts—and observes how our dissection of such concepts has, in many ways, made these ideas both difficult to understand and confusing. He notes that we make a mistake when we stray into the 'minefield of potential misconception and general hazard'[19] surrounding the terms of 'sea power'.

We need to get away from entrenched and nuanced terms and focus on the obligation and the need to secure national objectives in the maritime domain. We now must think deeply about the strategic utility of concepts such as sea control and sea denial for contemporary and prospective naval and maritime power.

The fact is, sea control is increasingly out of the reach of modern navies. Nevertheless, where contemporary sea power comprehends decisive lethality as the ultimate sanction against the adversary's attempt to access focal areas, the desired strategic effect is achieved. This is the whole point of sea power.

To understand how the Navy contemplates its core roles in realising the tasks that government might require it to undertake, it is important to understand the nature of naval power.

In the March–April 1974 edition of *The Naval War College Review*, VADM Stansfield Turner, the former distinguished President of what continues to be one of the world's pre-eminent naval institutions, published a major paper entitled 'Missions of the US Navy'. Before getting to the substance of his paper, Turner set an ongoing challenge: to look carefully at which of our missions best suit the tenor of the times. He said that we should 'take stock of our purpose in life in order to allocate the diminishing resources available to us in the best possible way'.[20] This task is no less relevant today than it was forty years ago.

Turner displayed a deep appreciation of the writings of Alfred Thayer Mahan whose work at the US Naval War College saw him promoted to Rear Admiral upon his retirement. In 1890, Mahan published his groundbreaking study *The Influence of Sea Power upon History 1660–1783* in which he developed his concept of naval power as a critical component of both national economic strength and national strategic defence. As a strategic imperative, 'command of the sea' was succinctly expressed by Sir Walter Raleigh, who wrote 'whosoever commands the sea commands the trade; whosoever commands the trade of the world commands the riches of the world, and consequently the world itself'.[21] Although, so far as I can recall, Mahan did not himself use the term 'command of the sea', he implicitly identified 'sea power' as the instrument by which a nation exercised 'command of the sea'.

Mahan had an innate sense of political power as the driving force of national strategy. For him, 'sea power' was inseparable from the power of the state. Mahan wrote:

It is the possession of that overbearing power on the sea which drives the enemy's flag from it, or allows it to appear only as a fugitive; and

which, by controlling the great common [the ocean], closes the high-
ways by which commerce moves to and from the enemy's shores.[22]

This is an important observation, not least of all because it ties the use
of naval power firmly to the ability of the state to maintain its economic
strength and the well-being of its citizens. This was a point that Grand
Admiral von Tirpitz, the architect of the imperial German Navy and a dis-
ciple of Mahan, understood only too well. The withdrawal of the German
High Seas Fleet following the Battle of Jutland was a significant contributor to Germany's economic decline and eventual defeat.

Geoffrey Till notes another critically important feature of Mahan's
thinking that has in many respects become a more important contributor
to effective maritime power—the quality of the people who fight our ships:

> There was, in many of Mahan's books, a strong focus on battle between
> concentrations of heavy warships as the ultimate decider of naval power.
> The outcome of battle depended not merely on the quality of the ships
> present, however, but on training, morale, the effectiveness of command,
> tactical disposition (in particular) skill in pitting all your force against a
> portion of the opponent's (and), above all on an offensive spirit—the
> desire to close and destroy.[23]

As a serious student of Mahan's thinking, Turner described four corner-
stones of contemporary naval power—strategic deterrence, sea control,
projection of power ashore and naval presence—which remain as true
today as they were in 1974. What has changed, however, is the balance
between these core missions and the strategic context within which we
seek to achieve them. That lethality is the key to our nations' ability to
wage war has not changed. But how we deploy and deliver that lethality
has changed enormously.

Like Mahan, Turner had a deep appreciation of the relationship between
the state as a political entity and the Navy as a principal vehicle for policy
delivery in troubled times. Our elected governments and the worried tax-
payers they represent are dazzled by costs. But they have an unswerving
ability to judge the value of what they pay for. So this essay is intended, in

part, to set out the arguments supporting the demands Navy places on the public purse in terms of the strategic benefits the Navy delivers. In other words, this essay is, in part, a recalibration of Turner's central premises in the light of current and prospective strategic circumstances.

The global strategic pre-eminence of the US is currently contested in a way that Turner could not have imagined when he wrote his essay. Turner's navy was, in his words, recuperating from the wounds of Vietnam. The contemporary USN is contemplating the consequences of the wars in Iraq and Afghanistan, and the ongoing conflicts in the Middle East. Each of the Allies that continue to support policies aimed at stabilising the Middle East and Afghanistan shows signs of the fatigue that impacts on popular support for prolonged engagement in distant theatres.

We are seeing new challenges to the rule of law, from both state and non-state actors, using threat vectors that are new and different.

The concepts that underpin the 'freedom of the seas', as encapsulated by the great Dutch jurist Hugo Grotius in the seventeenth century, and on which maritime law has been founded ever since, are under threat as never before. We need only to consider the contemporary tensions in the South China Sea to appreciate how historic assumptions can so quickly be brought into dispute. And we are all confronted by the fracture of joint political and economic purpose in Europe, which could, in the extreme, result in the consequent erosion of joint strategic purpose.

Just as we have seen the gradual contraction of the RN, so we are witnessing the progressive rise of China as a global strategic power, and its ability to project its power at sea. China is working towards a blue water navy with access to both the Pacific and Indian Oceans. We are also witnessing the rise of India as a significant maritime power in the Indian and Pacific Oceans.

At the same time, Turner's real and present strategic threat—the Soviet Union—has been overtaken by a broader range of strategic threats, from states seeking to overturn the existing rule of law, from states seeking an outlet to nationalism, and from non-state actors who challenge the existence of states and their secular values. And the Soviet Union's successor, Russia, pursues adventurist policies that defy conventional ways of transacting international business. Moreover, we are learning to deal with the asymmetric threat of terrorism, which successfully impinges on the confidence of the electorate, and in Africa and the Middle East, seeks to replace states with a fourteenth-century model of autocratic power.

The great American novelist Mark Twain allegedly said, 'History does not repeat itself, but it does rhyme'. There are sufficient similarities between now and 1914 to warn us against strategic irresponsibility or inattention.[24]

It would be a bold national leader who, confronted by the uncertainties, ambiguities and discontinuities of the contemporary strategic situation, dismissed the ability to wage war as a thing of the past. It is perhaps unfashionable to talk about waging war as a core capability of a democratic state: it seems at one level to be incompatible with the rule of law, itself based on the value of the human person. But at another level, it seems to be inevitable, since the central duty of any democratic government is to uphold and defend the liberties that are expressed in the rule of law.

There are two propositions that merit a brief exploration if we are to recalibrate Turner's prescriptions: Clausewitz's 'war is the continuation of policy by other means'; and Bismarck's 'politics is the art of the possible'.

It has become something of a commonplace for 'war' to mean sustained action against something that we do not like: the war against illiteracy, the war against poverty, the war against disease.

But for those of us in the business of war, it has a much more terrible meaning. War is the sustained use of extreme violence by politics. War is the most serious social act available to human beings. War is a cataclysmic political upheaval: a devastating physical event, which marks the bounds between societies.[25] This is why the war against Islamic terrorism is so transfixing and so critical. The corollary is—as Clausewitz would have it—that the ability to wage war is intrinsic to the nature of the state, and the survival of the state.

If war is thus understood, as Clausewitz described it, as 'the continuation of policy', we need to ask ourselves the question 'what is policy anyway?' Essentially, policy comprehends the principles on which leaders take decisions in the interests of the state and its citizens.

Diplomacy is the conduct of relations between independent states on the basis of intelligence and tact, as Sir Ernest Satow reminds us in his *Guide to Diplomatic Practice*—the training manual for young diplomats in years past.[26] Unfortunately, however, while diplomacy is a necessary component in the conduct of international relations, it is not sufficient. Historically, resort to armed force has remained an option for many national leaders, to the immense cost to their communities.

War is the conduct of relations between independent political bodies when intelligence and tact have been replaced by belligerence and aggression. War and peace look very different. But there is no sharp break between peace and war. It is possible, as the events of 1914 establish, to sleepwalk into war. War becomes inevitable when peace cannot be maintained and pursued. Peace is not the absence of war. Rather, it is the other way round: war is the inevitable consequence when peace disappears.

Clausewitz understood the peace–war spectrum—that a state's ability to maintain and preserve the peace extends to its ability to wage war. But the spectrum is not linear: rather, it is characterised by political and strategic ambiguity, and fundamental discontinuities as leaders take decisions without a full appreciation of risk. Consequently, deterrence, in Turner's conception of the term, only has meaning if the state is able to address the failure of deterrence by employing lethality that is both strategic and proportionate. So the ability to wage war is a core element of 'continuity' in policy.

But Clausewitz goes much further. War is not just the continuation of policy. It is the continuation of policy 'by other means'. Without the ability to wage war, the state is unable to 'continue policy'. In other words, without the ability to wage and win war, the state fails to fulfil the central demand on it—to ensure the protection of its citizens and its own existence. The constant that underpins the state's ability to continue policy by other means is the armed force available to it, and its willingness to use that force.

Governments are always reluctant to spend their treasure and to risk spilling the blood of their citizens. They should be reluctant. As the history of the twentieth century demonstrates so conclusively, war brings with it death and destruction, grief and pain. But precisely because the future is unpredictable and the events that lead to war so chaotic, no government that values its citizens and defends their freedom can ignore the awful dynamics of armed conflict. The power to address the demands of armed conflict and the resolution to do so are elements of state power that Churchill understood well. Reflecting on the Agadir crisis of 1911, when imperial Germany deployed SMS *Panther* and SMS *Berlin* to sanction the French

Army's expansion into the Moroccan interior, Churchill condemned the complacency of peacetime. He wrote with withering irony:

> So now the Admiralty wireless whispers through the ether to the tall masts of ships, and captains pace their decks absorbed in thought. It is nothing. It is less than nothing. It is too foolish, too fantastic to be thought of in the twentieth century. Or is it fire and murder leaping out of the darkness at our throats, torpedoes ripping the bellies of half-awakened ships, a sunrise on a vanished naval supremacy, and an island well-guarded hitherto, at last defenceless? No, it is nothing. No one would do such things. Civilization has climbed above such perils. The interdependence of nations in trade and traffic, the sense of public law, the Hague Convention, Liberal principles, the Labour Party, high finance, Christian charity, common sense have rendered such nightmares impossible. Are you quite sure? It would be a pity to be wrong. Such a mistake could only be made once—once for all.[27]

When he wrote this in 1923 with characteristic resonance, Churchill was looking back at Agadir through the lens of our joint experience of World War I. And perhaps now it is even more the case that maritime power resides at the heart of our ability to remain independent and free. Independence and freedom are the values that underpin our democracies. They are also the values on which our alliances are built, a point that we shall deal with a little further into this essay.

So, what is the defining element of a state's ability to wage war?

As was mentioned earlier, the defining element is lethality. This is the central concept that allows us to recalibrate Turner's four core prescriptions. This is because deterrence, sea control, power projection and naval presence are all consequences of the state's ability to deliver strategic lethality. And this is where the 'art of the possible' comes into play: by ensuring the dedicated availability of lethality within the panoply of state power, it remains possible for the state to wage war, and hence to maintain the practice of politics. In that ultimate sense, politics is only possible when the employment of lethal force remains a consideration.

I want to demonstrate this theoretical approach in a practical example. As a young officer filling an exchange posting with the RN in 1982, I saw firsthand the UK's deployment of naval power to retake the Falklands (known to the Argentineans, in Spanish, as the Islas Malvinas), itself a consequence of a profound strategic miscalculation by Argentinean President Leopoldo Galtieri.

The key to the UK's success was a demonstration of strategic lethality, and an ability to prosecute decisive lethality. The sinking of ARA *General Belgrano* by HMS *Conqueror* was an exercise in strategic lethality. Sadly for *Belgrano*, formerly the USS *Phoenix*, there was no rising from the ashes. Lethality was decisive and total. The continued delivery of decisive lethality against Argentinean forces on the Falkland Islands and in its sea approaches determined the outcome of the war. Lethality was the cause, and defeat was the consequence. So also were sea control, power projection and naval presence. Similarly, the deployment of USS *Carl Vinson* in the Arabian Sea–Persian Gulf during 2015 delivered decisive lethality against the IS forces in northern Iraq.

The days when the USN could deploy invincible force globally are receding. Just as the strategic supremacy of the US is contested, so too is the power of the USN. Mass is no longer the determining factor, although, as Stalin said, 'quantity has a quality all of its own'. For twenty-first-century naval power, the determining factor is the ability to deliver the kind of lethality that destroys the adversary's command and control—that is, strategic lethality—or prevents the adversary from the exercise of armed force to secure its strategic objective—that is, decisive lethality.

So long as strategy embraces the need for lethal force to hopefully deter, and ultimately to defeat the enemy, the failure of deterrence is never the failure of strategy.

The lens through which we need to view sea control is the lens of domain exploitation for maximum strategic effect—capitalising on the adversary's vulnerability in order to defeat him. Similarly, the strategic effect delivered by Turner's power projection mission is equally well delivered when the state's strategic systems (in the case of the US, the ballistic missile nuclear submarines and the strategic air command) are able to deter and defeat possible adversaries.

And the strategic effect of the fourth of Turner's missions—naval presence—is delivered when the undetected and, we hope, undetectable elements of the naval force-in-being constrain the adversary's freedom of action. This gestures to the swing that has taken us away from target- or threat-centred strategies to vulnerability-centred strategies where the targets are less important than the exploitation of vulnerability and the denial of opportunity.[28] This is precisely the strategic offensive role of submarines—to exploit the vulnerability of the adversary at the point of greatest vulnerability.

Decisive and distributed lethality

Lethality is the business of the armed forces, and lethality at sea is the business of the Navy. Lethality is not just about rendering inoperable the forces of the adversary. It is about affecting the adversary's capacity for making decisions. Is the inevitable loss of life acceptable or unacceptable? Is the inevitable loss of platforms acceptable or unacceptable? This is what we might describe as 'messing with the adversary's mind'. So decisive lethality is the use of proportionate armed force to constrain the ability of the adversary to decide—in effect, to exercise command. And for moderate-sized navies such as the RAN and the RN, lethality is applied at a particular point where the adversary is most vulnerable. To that degree, decisive lethality is a tactical concept.

For the USN, however, lethality has a much broader connotation, since lethality is applied across a multiplicity of systems and domains to deliver strategic effects. In that sense, distributed lethality is a strategic concept. And decisive lethality, as generated by the RAN and the RN, is the necessary precursor to the distributed lethality that is the strategic focus of the USN today. Moreover, the ability of both the RAN and the RN to operate asymmetrically—especially with respect to our submarine operations—delivers sea denial as a critical strategic effect. And this, by the way, goes to the fundamental significance of our alliance with the US.

So what does 'sea control' mean for naval operations in the twenty-first century? When Turner coined the term, he was recalibrating and providing contemporary meaning to the more ambitious concept 'sea power', as articulated by Mahan. This was a static concept that, in Mahan's day, did not address the increasing dynamism of the war at sea afforded by new technologies and new operational concepts, both driven by new and different political purposes. Turner intended a 'more realistic control in limited areas and for limited periods of time'. As he said in 1974, 'It is conceivable today to exert air, submarine, and surface control temporarily in an area while moving ships into position to project power ashore or to resupply overseas forces'.[29]

Importantly, conflicts such as the Falklands War demonstrated that a static approach to sea power was no longer viable, if it ever was. Capabilities able to exploit the sea in one domain (for instance the RN's SSNs in the underwater domain) denied the Argentinean forces their ability to exploit the sea using capabilities optimised for other domains (for instance surface warships exploiting the sea surface domain). The strategic result was to confound Argentina's political decision-making. The RN messed with President Galtieri's mind.

His was not the only mind that the RN messed with. As the late Admiral Sandy Woodward RN pointed out, Britain's SSNs were influential in the outcome of the Falkland's campaign well before the *Belgrano* was sunk. The Argentineans were planning to invade the islands in September 1982. But when a British SSN departed Gibraltar earlier in the March of the same year, Rear Admiral Anaya, the Argentinean commander, believed the British had caught wind of the invasion plans and that, once the SSN was stationed in the South Atlantic, the RN had a sufficient force structure that could sustain an SSN presence indefinitely—forever foiling an Argentinean invasion plan. So they went early, and the rest is history. Woodward's example truly captures the essence of sea denial, as decisive lethality impacted the political mind. Rear Admiral Anaya had his mind messed with, too.

As an aside, Admiral Woodward wryly noted the British SSN dived on exiting the Mediterranean and turned north! Such is the advantage of stealth and ambiguity inherent in submarines—it messes with the enemy's mind.

Turner never envisaged sea control as the static domination of maritime spaces by overwhelming naval force, not least of all because that force itself becomes the victim of spatial control rather than controlling the dynamics of the battle at sea. But for many commentators and writers, 'sea control' has become a strategic end in itself rather than a tool for victory. This is to recall an earlier point. The terms of sea power can become dogmatised and unconstructive. As an established—and largely unchallenged term—'sea control' is an idea that reflects the musings of a long period of peace, but it is not necessarily the pragmatic concept necessary for winning the war at sea.

This is not to suggest that we dismiss established concepts such as 'sea control' out of hand. Rather, we need to give them contemporary and practical application. That is twofold: first, we need to retain the ability to exploit and manipulate the strategic advantages deriving from our ability to project power at sea; and second, we particularly need to look to our strategic capacity for allied and coalition operations to ensure that we have the mass and the flexibility to gain and hold control of the sea.

This is where interdependence and partnership come into their own—an issue addressed later in this essay.

It is absolutely critical that we maintain our focus on the cardinal capabilities that enable us to apply lethal force at the adversary's point of maximum vulnerability, where the application of that lethal force makes the greatest strategic sense. There are five cardinal capabilities.

First, force projection at a distance, as was demonstrated during the Battle of the Coral Sea.

Second, the imposition of unacceptable costs, as was demonstrated at the Battle of Jutland.

Third, targeted and decisive lethality, as was demonstrated by the RN during the Falklands War, and by the USN during the First Iraq War.

Fourth, agility, by which is meant the ability to take decisions quickly, to manoeuvre naval force with speed and flexibility, and to enhance survivability by ensuring that our war fighters are able to adapt doctrine and tactics to meet the needs of the moment, as was demonstrated during the Battle of Leyte Gulf.

And finally, the 'exploitation' and 'manipulation' of the sea as the dynamic contemporary meaning of the traditional static concept of 'sea control,' which is what the RN eventually achieved in the Battle of the Atlantic.

The lesson for the Navy is clear: we need to look beyond the constraints imposed on our ability to acquire and retain advanced systems by rising technology costs and the increasing demands on the national purse.

This is the critical test of leadership—the ability to inform and strengthen our governments in setting clear strategic direction and providing the wherewithal to achieve that strategic direction, and to empower our fleet commanders and the captains of our warships to exercise their imaginations and initiative within the framework of clear strategic direction.

And, as we celebrate the eight hundredth anniversary of the signing of *Magna Carta*, we need to remind ourselves once again of what war is all about. It is ultimately about deterring, resisting and defeating any attack on the freedoms and values that define us as nations. And, in this sense, as we saw with the 9/11 attacks on the US and the current activities of the IS forces in northern Iraq, an attack on any one of the allied democracies is an attack on all of them. So for those of us who are the descendants of Westminster—Australia, Canada and New Zealand, and the US, if I might make free with some aspects of colonial history—we need to see that our ability to act in the common defence of our values goes to the heart of twenty-first-century naval power.

THE STRATEGIC CONTEXT

NOBODY CONTESTS THE fact that we live in interesting times. Equally uncontested is the fact that we live in confusing times, where despotic and inequitable governments and anarchic and terrorist splinter groups combine to erode public confidence in the values that unite the great democracies. The tragedy of 9/11, the Madrid bombings in 2004, the London bombings in 2005, the incident in the Canadian Parliament in 2014, the terrorist incidents in Paris and Copenhagen in 2015, and the terrorist attack by a lone gunman in Orlando, Florida, in 2016 remind us that democratic governments and publics everywhere feel insecure and under threat.

When our security is under threat, so too are the values that define us as societies—the values that, as noted earlier in this essay, we sum up in the expression 'rule of law' and that President Roosevelt described in his Four Freedoms speech seventy-five years ago. These are the freedoms upon which the cohesion and stability of the nations that navies serve are based. As servants of the state, it is the business of our armed forces to protect and defend these freedoms. And for leaders of the RAN, the task is to refresh the Navy's understanding of the principles on which our Services are founded. More than that, it is to ensure that those principles have contemporary meaning and relevance.

Successive Defence White Papers have analysed the strategic environment within which the Australian Defence Force operates. While these
White Papers have charted the currents and eddies of strategic change at
both the global and regional level, they have concluded that the regional
environment is generally benign. They have also noted, however, that change
can occur quickly.

Strategic change is often the result of fundamental discontinuities occur-
ring where the political, economic and social domains intersect, where the
knock-on effects of dislocation at one level impact on another. Whether
that is significant leadership change, as occurs when a country is subject to
a *coup d'état*, or sudden economic change resulting in popular dislocation,
strategic instability is always just around the corner. For this reason, even
in times of relative peace, prudent governments maintain the capacity to
mount their self-defence against armed aggression or the threat of armed
aggression. The defence of the nation's legitimacy and authority in the
twenty-first century depends on its ability to project strategic lethal force
over, on and beneath the sea.

And lethality is the key to our ability to wage war. This is the central
driver of all defence capability planning: the ability to inflict unacceptable
losses on an adversary to deter the use of armed force and, if that fails, to
defeat the adversary in armed combat.

Australia has the enormous good fortune both to occupy a continent
and to enjoy a geographic location far from the traditional centres of human
conflict. But while we might be far from the historical theatres of war, our
national interests are deeply entrenched in the maintenance of global stability
and the orderly operation of international commerce. Australia's prosperity is
dependent on foreign direct investment, itself critical to our ability to exploit
our natural resources and trade actively on international markets. Just as our
major trading partners such as China, Korea and Japan are dependent on our
coal, LNG and iron ore exports, so too are we dependent on fuel imports
from Singapore and technology imports (including motor vehicles) from
Europe and the US. And all of this trade is seaborne.

While our geography contributes significantly to our security and our
prosperity, it also positions us well to share in the growth and prosperity
that 'the Asian century' is delivering to the western Pacific. China's growth

in particular has contributed significantly to our prosperity over the past quarter century, and will continue to do so. China is, in fact, the major economic engine on which the global community increasingly depends for its economic well-being. At the same time, China's growth brings with it an inevitable change in the global power balance as its economic strength is increasingly matched by its strategic and political strength. As a dominant regional and global power, it is important that China is fully engaged in the maintenance of regional stability and security. To that end, China clearly has a place at the table that sets and monitors the rules by which the international community conducts its business and, equally, has a responsibility to observe those rules. That is the whole point of a 'rules-based system' that is such a key centrepiece in the 2016 Defence White Paper.

There has been much commentary on China's establishment of permanently manned facilities on a number of the atolls, reefs and cays in the South China Sea. With a multiplicity of claimants, these are contested waters. The only reasonable way to resolve the maritime boundary dispute is for the claimants, including China, to negotiate an agreement on seabed boundaries and on the appropriate exploitation of both fish stocks and seabed resources. Pre-emptive colonisation of the disputed reefs, the positioning of military assets, the declaration of exclusion zones and aggressive patrolling are not consistent with respect for a rules-based system.

In mid-2016, the Permanent Court of Arbitration in The Hague rejected critical elements of Beijing's claim over waters in the South China Sea. This ruling, which has endorsed the importance of a rules-based global order for the global maritime commons, suggests the need for restraint and preparedness to agree a resolution that accounts for the ruling.

A negotiated settlement is critical, since the sea lines of communication (SLOCs) that pass through the South China Sea are as important to China as an importer of raw materials as they are to Saudi Arabia and the Gulf States as exporters of crude oil, or Australia as an exporter of mineral and agricultural commodities.

As Mahan so clearly understood, seaborne commerce and naval power are meshed together: merchant vessels provide the business of the sea, and naval vessels provide the security of the sea. For that reason, the RAN is a key and inevitable component of our long-term trade security. Like our immediate neighbours and our traditional allies, Australia has a vested interest in the freedom of navigation and the peaceful use of the oceanic commons. While collaboration and cooperation with the navies of our friends and allies are essential features of SLOC protection, they can only be as successful as the contribution of each of the parties permits. Successive Australian governments have recognised that fact as the *sine qua non* of the nation's naval power.

Much of our minerals trade passes through the major Indonesian straits, Lombok and Sunda. Australia's strategic planners have long understood what history taught us in the twentieth century—that a direct attack on Australia can only come from or through the Indonesian archipelago, since a sea invasion on the east coast of Australia would be too difficult, too risky and practically insupportable from a logistic point of view. The curious 'confrontation' of 1963–66 aside (and it is important to understand that Australia was not the target of the *konfrontasi*, but rather the newly formed Federation of Malaysia), Australia has enjoyed sound diplomatic and defence relations with Indonesia. There have been political ups and downs, of course, which the fundamental structure of the relationship has weathered well. A stable and prosperous Indonesia is a great strategic asset to Australia. For that reason, our two navies cooperate well, with high-level policy discussions and joint exercises conducted on a regular basis.

While Asia's strategic outlook is reasonably benign, tensions can arise with little warning. North Korea is a country where unpredictability and impetuosity take the place of reason and caution, threatening not only South Korea but also its major neighbours, Japan and China. Japan remains locked in overlapping contests with China and Russia concerning disputed territories, and while China and Taiwan remain unable to agree on what 'one China' actually means, the possibility of serious disagreement remains alive. And, of course, China will continue to contest the maritime dominance of the US in the Pacific, with the possibility of escalation if the potential for shouldering and other aggressive manoeuvres at sea are not tightly controlled. Similarly, careless or aggressive manoeuvres by patrol aircraft in the South China Sea and the Sea of Japan can trip tension.

The combination of protecting seaborne trade and managing the unexpected provides the key strategic underpinning of Australia's naval power. Any serious outbreak of tension in the north Pacific would immediately involve Australia's security interests, a fact that has engaged the attention of successive governments, and will continue to preoccupy future governments. The ability to mount effective defensive operations against armed force and an appropriate offensive capability to 'mess with the adversary's mind' will remain key strategic imperatives for Australia, and the key responsibility of the RAN.

ALLIANCES AND COALITIONS

THE COMMUNITY OF western nations emerged from the Cold War with a feeling of strategic vindication and a strong sense of relief. Our governments immediately began harvesting the 'peace dividend', channelling spending away from defence into the national social and physical infrastructure. The focus of strategic planning moved from collective defence to national defence. Alliances, of course, stayed in place, while unwieldy treaties such as SEATO and CENTO had already fallen into abeyance. We all hoped that we would never again need to prepare for all-out war.

But here again hope triumphed over experience.

Through the nineties we saw a number of peacekeeping operations in Kuwait, Angola, Cambodia, Somalia, Rwanda, the Balkans and East Timor, to name just a few. These operations reflected growing international concern with human security issues, and demonstrated yet again that the prevention of war, the enforcement of the peace and the maintenance of stability are cooperative endeavours. And, as was mentioned earlier, 9/11 saw the community of liberal democracies come together in ways that were unprecedented.

In the twenty-first century, the world community faces international terrorism on a scale unimaginable in the twentieth century. The long engagements in Iraq and Afghanistan have seen the democracies come together in coalitions that are focused as much on national security as they are on global security, the return of stability to Iraq and Afghanistan and the defeat of terrorist groups.

For Australia, our traditional alliances have strengthened in the last decade or so. Our long-standing relationships with the UK, the US and New Zealand have provided the springboard for our cooperation with NATO partners. And in Asia, our relationships have diversified and strengthened in ways that were inconceivable a decade or so ago. We are increasingly aware of the interdependence that is central to the ability of modern states to manage their broader regional and global security interests. The emergence of new strategic players, changing strategic balances and the shifting kaleidoscope of interests and aspirations is creating a multidimensional strategic environment where new forms of partnership and cooperation emerge to address the protection and promotion of common interests. Whereas alliances are relationships with 'lock in', these emerging partnerships and coalitions are flexible, adjusting quickly both to problems and to opportunities.

But, from the viewpoint of war fighting, alliances and partnership are the essential preconditions of distributed lethality. They are the critical factors for transcending the limits of decisive lethality, driven by national capability, to enable distributed lethality, driven by common purpose. There are three counterpart navies with which the RAN has enjoyed long and close association, and it worth examining quickly how these traditional linkages work to mutual advantage.

Working with the USN

In 1908, just eight months after Prime Minister Deakin had delivered his speech on naval policy in the House of Representatives, referred to earlier in this essay, the US Fleet visited Sydney, Melbourne and Albany. The visit of the Great White Fleet, as it came to be known, was a direct result of Deakin's invitation to President Theodore Roosevelt. In this, both the Admiralty and the Colonial Office were unwilling to support Deakin's initiative, but Deakin proceeded anyway. Deakin had two main purposes in hosting the Great White Fleet: first, he wanted to emphasise the interdependence of a buoyant and growing trading economy and naval power—something the US understood implicitly as a result of Mahan's work. And second, he wanted the Australian people to see what a real fleet looked like. Apart from the cruiser HMS *Powerful*, the flagship, the RN's Imperial Squadron, based in Sydney, consisted of mainly obsolete ships, all of which could be withdrawn at any time to meet other imperial tasks should they arise.

The Great White Fleet was a sensation. At a time when Sydney's population was barely six hundred thousand, half a million people turned out to view the ships. The impact was immediate, and Deakin made his point. As he commented at the time, 'We live in hopes that from our own shores some day a fleet will go out not unworthy to be compared in quality, if not in numbers, with the magnificent fleet now in Australian waters'.[30] The visit of the US fleet had a number of important consequences. First, the Australian Parliament, with Deakin in the driver's seat, set about the acquisition of Australian fleet units to undertake the nation's coastal defence. Second, probably to keep the fledgling Australian naval interests in the imperial corner, the Admiralty agreed to the exchange of naval personnel that has been part of the RAN's ongoing links with the RN for more than a century. Third, it brought the First Sea Lord, Admiral Sir John Fisher, into play, resulting in Australia's decision to acquire HMAS *Australia*, the first of our capital ships. As David Stevens notes:

> On 4 October 1913 the first flagship, the battlecruiser HMAS *Australia*, and her escorts sailed into Sydney Harbour to a welcome no less enthusiastic than that accorded the Great White Fleet five years before. Just ten months later the fleet set out to face the harsh test of a brutal global war and its professionalism was not found wanting. For a newly acquired navy it was a remarkable achievement, and one which owed much to Deakin's foresight.[31]

World War II initiated a complete reorientation in Australia's strategic policy. Following the fall of Singapore, Prime Minister Curtin set about rebuilding Australia's global strategic relationships from the ground up. As the account of the Battle of the Coral Sea earlier in this essay observed, the USN and the RAN worked hand in glove throughout the Pacific war. This was not a function simply of necessity or of opportunity. Rather, it was a partnership built around long-term strategic objectives—objectives that endure today. The ANZUS treaty, signed in the aftermath of the allied victory in the Pacific, gives formal expression to the alliance. But, like all formal expressions, it is only as good as the actions and the outcomes it generates. And this is where ANZUS has proved itself to be a remarkable strategic relationship. Because the treaty enjoys the fullest support at the highest levels of both the Australian and US governments, the RAN has unparalleled access to the systems and doctrine of the USN. Not only do our fleet units work together seamlessly, we also share systems and information at the highest levels of national classification.

Examples help. At one point, when the US Deputy Chief of Naval Operations was in Canberra, the Collins class submarine project was experiencing complications. Within very short order, our ally put forward a team of senior US naval officers—submariners and engineers—to offer whatever support the RAN needed, including access to the most advanced facilities of the US submarine force. The issues were resolved—we now have one of the world's most effective, large conventional submarines. This is the kind of alliance cooperation that flows from common and constant strategic purpose which, for both Australia and the US, centres on the defence of those values we hold in common: freedom, the rule of law, and democratic rights.

Notwithstanding the disparity in the size of our populations—the US is over twenty times bigger than Australia and one state, California, has an economy bigger than ours—we both bring to the table important qualities and capabilities that enhance the strategic position of both parties. Nor should anyone underestimate the value deriving from differences between the capabilities of the RAN and the USN. As Geoffrey Till has noted: 'the issue of the extent to which navies are "different" is important because the answer has a bearing on what special capabilities they have to offer and on the extent to which, and the manner in which, they operate alongside the other services'.[32] As the US and Australia face, together, the opportunities and uncertainties of this 'Pacific century', cultural affinity, single-mindedness and the practical strength that comes from partnership, will be critical in overcoming what Geoffrey Blainey famously labelled the 'tyranny of distance'.

Coining this phrase, Blainey gestured to the way in which geographical isolation contributed to the formation of an Australian national identity. But remoteness and distance also exert a critical influence upon the constructive and special relationship between the USN and the RAN. This is a partnership informed by a common heritage, values and history, energised by a commitment to global good order and formalised in our long-standing alliance.

The strength of the bilateral defence relationship between our two countries will grow. The entry into service of new surface and subsurface vessels, all of them equipped with shared communications, sensors, fire control systems and weapons, will further embed a habit of cooperation to the advantage not just of both parties, but to the advantage of the entire Pacific community.

Working with the RN

This essay began with a brief account of the RAN's heritage. Australia's Navy is, in important ways, an offspring of the RN. I am not the only Australian naval officer whose father was an officer in the RN, as well as the RAN. Australia has inherited many of its naval traditions from the RN. As an imperial power, Britain effectively dominated the nineteenth century. And the RN was at the very centre of British imperial power.

Rudyard Kipling had a poetical style somewhat reminiscent of that of the great Australian balladeer, C.J. Dennis. In his poem *Mandalay*, he wrote (in the voice of an Eastender, one suspects):

> Ship me somewheres east of Suez, where the best is like the worst,
> Where there aren't no Ten Commandments an' a man can raise a thirst.

It would be a brave person who might suggest that British colonial policy was a reflection of Kipling's thinking, but there is no doubt that Kipling reflected many of the values that made Britain the colonial power it was. I am not sure, however, that ships' captains today would grant their crews a 'run ashore' where an absence of the Ten Commandments and thirst go hand in hand!

World War I eroded both the economic and strategic power of Great Britain, and World War II left Britain almost bankrupt. Its global footprint reduced progressively until, eventually, the Wilson government said 'enough is enough'. For a couple of decades following the decision of the Wilson government in 1968 to withdraw UK forces stationed 'east of Suez'—who would have thought that Defence Secretary Denis Healey would channel Kipling—opportunities for joint exercises, even under the Five Power Defence Arrangements, declined. In recent years, however, the relationship has strengthened as the defence forces of Australia and the UK work together in Iraq and Afghanistan to defeat global terrorism. Our armies and air forces, in particular, have benefited from the opportunity to operate together in pursuit of a common enemy once more—something they have been unable to do since the Malayan Emergency and Confrontation in the mid-sixties. Our two navies conduct high-level discussions, doctrinal and technical exchanges. We continue to exchange officers at all levels and from all specialties, which is one of the best ways of maintaining quality control in both our navies. We continue to exercise with RN fleet units whenever the opportunity arises. Like Australia, the UK is globally connected, and the economic and political development taking place in the western Pacific is of direct importance to the UK economy.

In view of the emerging complexities that increasingly distinguish the twenty-first century, the ability of our two navies to operate in joint and combined forces, including with the USN, will contribute enormously to the ability of the community of democratic nations to contain and defeat the forces of global terrorism.

Working with the RNZN

Australia's military and naval association with 'the Kiwis' predates Federation. Indeed, the flow of people between Australia and New Zealand before Federation was constant, and while many identified themselves as either one or the other, people joined together in common purpose, whether in agriculture, commerce, banking or the military forces. It is not widely known in Australia that Maori have been a presence in the Australian population since the early nineteenth century, with strong and thriving communities in regional Australia as well as in the cities. These links have endured across many generations.[33] And notwithstanding the All Blacks' domination in rugby and the bowling technique of the brother of a certain Australian cricket captain, there are no two nations that are closer in attitude, aptitude and affection than Australia and New Zealand.

ANZAC collaboration began well before the failed Dardanelles campaign. As many of the graves at Gallipoli attest, Kiwis enlisted enthusiastically in the first AIF, as did Australians in the New Zealand Expeditionary Force. The basic difference between the Australian and New Zealand contribution to the World War I allied effort was that New Zealand troops were allocated to British command, while forces of the first AIF remained under national command. This reflected New Zealand's somewhat closer alignment and identification with 'the mother country' than was the Australian disposition, regardless of the cries of 'For King and Country' that accompanied Australian recruiting campaigns.

While the RAN had already emerged from the RN's naval hatchery by the outbreak of war, the RNZN had a much longer incubation period, notwithstanding New Zealand's funding of the battle cruiser HMS *New Zealand*, which fought in the Battle of Jutland. In the inter-war years, the RN continued to provide vessels, officers and crew, with some New Zealand exchange personnel—all at New Zealand's expense. But while the RAN began to create its own identity separate from that of the RN, New Zealand naval personnel remained integrated with the RN until late in 1941, when the New Zealand Division of the RN became the RNZN. But personnel deployed to the European theatre remained embedded in the RN until the war's end.

The war in the Pacific, however, saw the gradual emergence of the RNZN as an independent naval force. The rebadged HMNZS *Achilles*, which had played such an important role in the defeat of the Nazi pocket-battleship *Admiral Graf Spee* in the Battle of the River Plate, and HMNZS *Leander* were seriously damaged in separate actions during the Guadalcanal campaign. RNZN minesweepers were also part of the allied force in the Pacific, and one, HMNZS *Kiwi* sank a Japanese submarine off Guadalcanal. What the RNZN might have lacked in size it certainly did not lack in courage or success.

But it was the aftermath of World War II that really brought the RAN and the RNZN together, under the auspices of the ANZUS treaty. Bilateral cooperation has been seamless ever since, even after the USN decided to suspend exercises in the mid-eighties as a result of the Lange government's decision to exclude nuclear-powered and/or nuclear-armed vessels from New Zealand's ports. The RNZN's cadets train with their RAN counterparts at the Australian Defence Force Academy, and embark on their post graduation specialist training together.

The construction of the ANZAC frigate, and the decision by the New Zealand government to acquire two—HMNZS *Te Kaha* and HMNZS *Te Mana*—brought new possibilities for interoperability. Yet, as the capabilities of the RAN's ANZACs have undergone upgrades and new capabilities have been installed, there are the beginnings of a divergence in the capabilities of our two navies. While Australia has placed its capability focus on high-end conflict—the new Air Warfare Destroyer, Wedgetail airborne early warning and control aircraft, the Joint Strike Fighter and the next generation submarines—New Zealand's capability focus is on its enormous exclusive economic zone, fisheries management, and the security of the island nations of the southwest Pacific. New Zealand has a long history of successful involvement in the southwest Pacific that other nations, including Australia, can only envy. The change in priority focus is a factor that neither the New Zealand nor the Australian Chief of Navy would allow to get in the way of the close relationship our navies have built up over the past seventy-five years. Our continued engagement and exchanges reflect a fundamental strategic fact: not only do Australia and NZ share fundamental values for which we have fought together in the past, we also have shared interests in the stability and security of our region extending from natural disasters to peacekeeping. But what is more, we share common interests in the maintenance of global strategic stability and order in which both our nations are heavily invested.

Interdependence and self-reliance

Strategic commentary abounds with myths. Many of them reflect a naïve linearity of thinking, while others indicate an inability on the part of the commentators to understand the systemic nature of both strategic policy and force posture. Self-reliance and interdependence do not sit at the ends of some kind of polar spectrum, locked in both competition and opposition. Nations spend their money on military systems to meet national objectives. Australia is no exception.

Our force posture is constructed to meet the specific strategic objectives ordained by government. Indeed, if our force posture were not so constructed, we would have a defence capability that consisted of little more than a mish-mash, an untidy kit bag of tools lacking purpose, focus and meaning. But it is precisely the coherence of our force posture, designed as it is to meet the imperatives of our national strategic goals, that enables Australia to contribute to and benefit from this strategic interdependence, not just with our traditional partners in Britain, New Zealand and the US, but with key Asian partners such as Japan, Singapore and Indonesia.

Strategy, as we know, is ultimately about ends and means. And where 'ends'—that is, strategic goals—are shared, 'means' enable the cooperation that is increasingly the engine for waging war. And just as self-reliance and interdependence do not exist as polar opposites, nor do 'ends' and 'means'. They are dynamic coefficients that mutually condition each other in decision-making. This has a fascinating consequence: interdependence is as much an 'end' in conceiving strategic success as it is a 'means' for delivering it. It is intrinsic to sound strategy.

By virtue of its history, its tradition, its doctrine and its culture, the RAN is well positioned for the demands of joint and combined operations with allies and partners. Cooperation and interoperability are, as it were, in our DNA as a Service. Because the RAN operates in a global, interconnected environment, our alliances and partnerships are what deliver the distributed lethality that reinforces the strategic effectiveness of our decisive lethality.

Managing relationships

Australian Chiefs of Navy would have a significantly reduced workload if the RAN were designed and structured to meet the more limited purposes of an exclusively national policy. A 'go it alone' navy would be considerably easier to command, not least of all because no consideration would need to be paid to the interests and abilities of others. But a 'go it alone' navy would also be useless. It would be a national albatross rather than a national asset. Central to the responsibilities of the Chief of Navy is the need to ensure that the RAN can interact with like-minded navies at the policy, planning and capability levels to deliver a better result. This is no simple task, but it is one that the ADF as a whole is actually very good at.

It may seem slightly odd to some that 'relationship management' would rank so high on the priorities of someone responsible for ensuring that the Navy is fit to fight wars. The development of trust and confidence, however, goes to the heart of the ability to deploy distributed lethality—to the heart of the ability to deny the maritime spaces to a would-be adversary.

We often talk about this in terms of 'interoperability'—the capacity to achieve similar goals employing similar capabilities. Consequently, modern military relationships focus as much on policy and doctrine as they do on operational techniques and tactical manoeuvres. While integrated command, control, communications and intelligence systems are the Holy Grail for many naval planners, their effect depends on the clarity of leadership intentions and the compatibility of doctrine—the principles upon which the Navy operates as a war-fighting system.

As Clausewitz famously noted, war is 'foggy'. 'War', he wrote, 'is the realm of uncertainty; three quarters of the factors on which action in war is based are wrapped in a fog of greater or lesser uncertainty'.[34]

In a world where 'fuzzy logic' is actually helping us to limit the consequences of uncertainty, it is hardly surprising that fixed systems, rigid thinking, inflexible rules and uniform procedures do not drive interoperability in contemporary and prospective circumstances. But where interoperability is based on the clarity of the goal and shared attachment to a common purpose, diversity in capabilities is no longer a showstopper. Indeed, capability diversity may well provide the additional force flexibility that takes 'messing with the adversary's mind' to new heights.

Strategic interdependence in the twenty-first century

The strategic challenges facing modern governments are enormous. The apparently chaotic nature of power shifts, related as they are to economic cycles, the forces of nationalism and ideology, the quality of international leaders and the resilience of communities, imposes extraordinary burdens on national governments.

In microcosm, the recent Greek debt crisis illustrates how uncertainty can work to threaten the destruction of a national economy and the destabilisation of the entire economy of Europe. Yet leaders recognised the need to support interdependence. If, in times of crisis, interdependence is so important, how much more important it is in times of opportunity. And, despite all the problems the international community is currently facing, there is enormous opportunity. Interdependence affords both leaders and planners a significant asset in the long-term enhancement of national, regional and global security, so long as they use it as a multiplier of national strategic capacity.

In 1907, Alfred Deakin saw interdependence in terms of Australia's place in the Empire, and its particular relationship with Britain. Yet he recognised interdependence for what it was—a fundamental strategic asset for those nations that put the value and dignity of their citizens at the centre of their national political, economic and strategic enterprise. One suspects that he would applaud those of his successors who have held a similar view and who have worked to deliver the range of alliances and partnerships that, for Australia, define our strategic interdependence, at the same time securing our strategic independence. For independence and interdependence are, as Deakin so clearly recognised, two sides of the same strategic coin.

THE NAVY AS A SYSTEM

IF THE NAVY is to redefine itself as a national enterprise, promoting and protecting the national interest alongside the Army and the Air Force, it is critically important that the Navy visualise itself as a fighting system. It cannot be just a collection of platforms or a breadth of capabilities ranging from humanitarian in their most benign form to lethal in their most offensive form. This is not, of course, an entirely novel idea—the most successful of our operational predecessors have grasped that instinctively. The point here is synergy as a core doctrinal concept, whereby decisive lethality is delivered by our entire system operating in a focused, networked and 'stitched up' way. This means that our civilian intelligence personnel, our dockyard workers, our naval architects, our enlisted and commissioned personnel act collectively to maximise the strategic effect of our platforms and their weapons systems. That system is further expanded in strategic effect when the Navy works jointly with the Army and the Air Force.

Traditionally, each of the Armed Services has been regarded as a collection of capabilities and platforms that can, in various combinations, provide government with a range of options to meet the defence imperatives of the day. This has generated two interesting consequences that, in combination, have tended to establish a platform-specific approach to force projection, on the one hand, and a replacement methodology in renewing the force structure on the other. As Andrew Gordon noted in *The Rules of the Game: Jutland and British Naval Command*, when operational planning becomes conventional, when doctrine becomes inflexible and command is exercised 'by the book', innovation, agility and flexibility are impossible.

Over the past two decades, much has been written on the topic of network-centric warfare, and much has been invested to ensure any given operational task can be conducted by the seamless interconnection of aircraft, ships, submarines and land forces to maximise the cost to the adversary's forces and minimise the exposure of our own forces. But network-centric systems are not standalone: their adaptability, agility and flexibility are a reflection of the people who operate and support them, and the technology on which they rely. This is an important consideration. To operate effectively, the Navy cannot set itself up as a 'closed system', functioning in isolation from the multitude of drivers that ultimately enable the system to achieve its purpose—decisive and distributed lethality. It has to operate as an 'open system', a fact that imposes challenges to traditional ways of doing things.

To meet the demands of twenty-first-century warfare, where the emphasis is on manoeuvre, agility, quick decision-making and the imposition of decisive lethality, the Navy needs to be seen as a thoroughly networked organism rather than a suite of separate capabilities, each one carefully compartmentalised and operating according to its own rules and procedures. A system is greater than the sum of its parts. But it is what makes it greater than the sum of its parts that is truly important: the trained and highly competent professionals who direct and operate it. Too often, systems are imagined in terms of machines with internal geometries and symmetries that deliver the same result in the same way every time, its quality control being measured in terms of flawless uniformity. Nothing could be further from the case. What makes a system both deliver what it is designed to deliver and adapt quickly to new demands is the intelligence that should be at the very starting point of design. And in the case of Navy, that intelligence is driven by our people—the 'human in the loop' as behavioural analysts are wont to say.

All systems have three major dimensions: the human dimension, the technological dimension and the organisational dimension. They are intimately connected, none functioning without the other two. So it is not simply that the 'human in the loop' matters. The 'human outside the loop' is just as important, as is the way that the humans both inside and outside the loop organise themselves.

The human dimension

Because the Navy is a national enterprise, the human dimension of the RAN system is both extensive and complex. It engages not only RAN personnel but also a vast network of specialists and individuals without whom the RAN simply could not operate. Alongside the members of our sister Services, these include the public servants who work within both the Navy strategic space and the Department of Defence to support the day-to-day management of the RAN, the naval reservists who contribute much value to our organisation, including much of our medical and legal staff requirements, public servants in both the federal and state jurisdictions who support the activities of the Navy in myriad ways, the many technical experts provided by private contractors, dockyard workers, engineering contractors, and, most importantly, the families of our naval members.

Our preoccupation with platforms and capabilities very often blinds us to the significant multiplier effect that can be generated when the human dimension of the system is fully integrated, and where each of the components of the human dimension can leverage the skills and abilities available across the entire system. There is considerable scope for improvement in the way that we engage with the people who are critical to our performance. Too often, we allow artificially constructed barriers between the various components of our extended workforce to impede progress. Too much time can be spent on repetitive negotiations between elements of our workforce, often at the cost of both performance and progress. Our workforce management needs to be seamless.

There are three aspects of personnel management that require particular attention if we are to meet the challenges of warfare in the twenty-first century: naval career management; skills integration between the RAN and the private sector; and an approach to enterprise management that favours partnership with critical technical and professional education providers in order to meet both contemporary and future skills challenges.

There is often a deep sense of disappointment and loss when skilled naval personnel leave the RAN for other, and sometimes greener, pastures. This is not simply a question of a haemorrhage of naval skills to the public or private sectors—that works entirely to the nation's benefit. Rather, the investment that the RAN makes in its people can be enhanced when they acquire professional and workforce experience in other sectors of the economy. What we presently lack is a way of attracting such people back into the Navy. But we do not lack the will to reform. This applies particularly to our people, very often women, who resign for family reasons, yet remain perfectly capable of both resuming and progressing their naval careers once their children begin attending school or other family issues have been resolved. Strong modern enterprises value their alumni, putting out a special welcome mat for those who might wish to return with broader skills and experience. While life at sea will remain largely a young person's career, the on-shore management of the Navy demands skilled and devoted people whose contribution is even greater to the extent that they understand the demands of the operational Navy at sea. Over the next few years, the RAN will be working to improve both its retention rate and, just as importantly, its return rate.

There is also a clear need for greater skills integration between the Navy and the private sector, whether by way of secondment of naval personnel to the private sector and *vice versa*, or the employment of private sector specialists through the naval reserve system. There are a number of specialist categories, particularly in engineering, where a greater focus on integration would be to the benefit of both the Navy and the private sector. In areas such as propulsion engineering, weapons engineering, communications and electronic engineering, our ability to maintain operational readiness and effectiveness would be enormously enhanced to the extent that skills, and the people with them, were transferable. We have been doing this successfully with the Defence Science and Technology Organisation—now the Defence Science and Technology Group—for years. What we need to do is to extend this practice to our private sector partners.

Core naval skills have changed enormously in the two and a quarter centuries that Australia has had a navy as part of its communications and defence. The fourteen-year-old powder monkeys on whom Nelson's fleet depended were rendered obsolete by the mechanised lifts that fed the turrets on the dreadnoughts. The duties of the sixteen-year-old gunsight-setter John Travers Cornwell VC, who died as a result of wounds sustained during the Battle of Jutland, are now fully automated, as are the duties of sailors like Australian Ordinary Seaman Teddy Sheean, who died while manning an anti-aircraft gun on HMAS *Armidale*, protecting his fellow crew members as they escaped their sinking ship on life rafts. And 'stokers'—among the toughest people in the Navy—have given way to automated engine management systems. In short, the core naval skills are no longer primarily physical. They are technical and intellectual.

As we look towards the future, particularly in the light of government decisions on the continuous build approach to platform acquisition, we should be acutely aware of the skills that we need as a nation to implement our fleet enhancement plans. We need to work with our universities and technology institutes to ensure that we have the professional skills to meet future demand. Whether in fields as distinct as naval architecture, advanced metallurgy, 3-D printing of specialised components, specialised welding, marine engineering or human factors analysis, industry in general and the Navy in particular are competing for skills in a restricted market. We need to take on our major educational institutions as partners to ensure that the national industry infrastructure is able to meet the demands that are now emerging. This is another area in which the Navy will be devoting additional energy over the next few years.

The technology dimension

In the hundred years since the Battle of Jutland, technology has developed in a way that would have been unimaginable to Admirals Jellicoe and Beatty, or Scheer for that matter. At Jutland, radiotelegraphy was only just replacing flags and lights as a means of communicating between ships. Gun laying was practised with trigonometry tables in hand, and range-finders were still a novelty. Ships were still coal powered. Aircraft were experimental. Technologies such as radar and sonar only emerged during World War II, when navigation was still done with sextant, chronometer and star chart. Surface to air missiles remained a naval futurist's dream.

Quite simply, technology's development is non-linear: it grows and changes differentially in all its domains. In just the past two decades, advances in solid-state physics, digitalisation, the chemistry of composites, miniaturisation and robotics, not to mention the satellite technology that enables GPS and ultra-high speed communications—the technological systems on which the RAN relies—have significantly enhanced the Navy's operational effectiveness. But as we look back over a fifty-year time frame, computing speeds have signalled perhaps the most significant technological expansion.

In 1965, Gordon Moore, in a short paper published in *Electronics* magazine, predicted that computing power would double every two years.[35] As *Scientific American* reported in 2015, Moore's Law (as it came to be known) has proved itself to be amazingly durable.[36] We are on the threshold, however, of Moore's Law finding itself in the dustbin of scientific history. While quantum computing is still in its infancy, recent breakthroughs in the US, Japan and Australia suggest that quantum computing may supersede the transistor-dependent electronic computer in the same way that digital computers made the Turing machine obsolete. Were quantum computing to provide the computational power to support developments in artificial intelligence, robotics and autonomous systems, the consequences for war fighting as we have known it historically are unimaginable.

But irrespective of the reasoning that might underpin as yet undiscovered technologies, there remain two critical aspects of war: it is the continuation of policy (in other words, it is a human artefact); and it takes place in space and time (in other words, sea, land and air remain critical dimensions for the conduct of warfare). This has three significant consequences for the Navy as a system.

First, no matter how advanced the technological dimension might be, and no matter how technically reliable 'fire and forget' weapons of the future might be, the human dimension remains integral for reasons of design, operation, decision, accountability, legality and morality. While the instruments of warfare may become more precise, their deployment incurring far less risk to our own combatants, their effects more proportional to the outcome mandated by the commander, and their lethality more decisive, they remain just that—instruments of war. Their use demands a decision-maker.

Second, no matter how great the inventory of smart weapons might be, targets are manifold. Not all targets are of equal value, and the prioritisation of targets will remain a key task, and a key accountability, of the commander. The human remains in the loop.

And third, war will always be the arena in which morality is most strenuously tested. Ethics and morality are at the centre of Navy's being: Navy's values are an expression of the core moral code that founds and energises an 'all volunteer' Service. The integrated system that constitutes the Navy, and the integrated system of systems that constitutes the ADF, cannot be left to independent programmed automata: they have to be deployed, the adversary has to be engaged, and the rules and conventions of armed conflict have to be observed. The system on which the conduct of warfare depends is a human artefact, as is war itself.

The organisational dimension

The human and technological dimensions of a system are integrated through organisational arrangements that maximise decision efficiency, weapons effectiveness, and the attainment of the strategic goal. Reflecting both advances in technology and the higher skill sets of its personnel, naval organisation has continued to evolve. In their earlier manifestations, navies were organised around capabilities and platforms, the structure of the fleet reflecting the various types of ships, submarines and aircraft available to the Fleet Commander. In recent years, however, naval organisation has tended to focus on the effects that the Navy is required to deliver. This approach maximises the commonalities that derive from integrated systems, and facilitates the flexibility and agility that are key to contemporary and prospective seapower.

In the maritime environment, success will increasingly depend on the ability of naval commanders to make decisions within the decision-loops of their adversaries—in other words, to beat them to the punch—and to deliver decisive lethality that deters or destroys the adversary's ability to take any further decisions.

Consequently, emergent naval organisation places a premium on flexibility, adaptability and agility. This demands constant innovation in organisational design, management and leadership. The importance of high quality professional development is highlighted by Geoffrey Till:

> An institutional culture in which the professional military education system (courses, staff training, reading material) helps develop naval personnel (both officers and ratings) interested in issues of innovation, skilled enough to analyse them effectively and ready to challenge defective ideas, irrespective of their origin. As a rule, an educated navy in which ideas are freely distributed and discussed performs better.[37]

And while, in disciplined Services such as the RAN, orders will still be orders, the emphasis for modern leaders will increasingly be on the empowerment of the team, the clarity of the objective, the constant improvement of skills, and the preservation of the core values that have traditionally driven the RAN—honour, honesty, courage, integrity and loyalty—all underpinned by the professionalism of every member of the RAN.

THE NAVY AS A NATIONAL ENTERPRISE

THE MOST SIGNIFICANT difference between the contemporary RAN and the Navy I joined forty years ago is that the Navy is increasingly embedded in the sinews and muscles of our nation. The Navy, as indeed the Army and the Air Force, is not just some kind of reserve national capability to be brought out in time of need, then put back into the cupboard of neglect. Rather, the Navy is an intrinsic national capability, intimately connected to the social, economic, industrial and educational drivers of national wellbeing. The modern Navy has to be a national enterprise, bringing together the private and public sectors of the economy to deliver a fundamental national objective—security above, on and under the sea. For the Navy to revisualise itself as a national enterprise—promoting and protecting the national interest—it is critically important that we see the Navy as a fighting system, not just as a collection of platforms.

Ultimately, government, as it acts in the interests of the nation, wants to deter conflict and contribute to the maintenance of peace and security around the world. It can only achieve that, however, if it is able to deploy lethality—or lethal capability—with decisive strategic effect to sanction anyone who might wish to use armed force against the nation or its interests. Lethality is the ultimate purpose of the Navy. Fear of the consequences deters armed adventurism since adventurism is deterred by the prospect of loss.

Lethality is the ability of Navy's fleet to generate decisive outcomes in conflict. This is relatively straightforward, though the word is often used without comprehending its implications for the manner in which we design, operate and sustain our maritime capabilities. Navies are a manifestation of purposeful government. And the defence of our nation's legitimacy and authority in the twenty-first century depends on our ability to project strategic lethal force over, on and beneath the sea—lethality is the key to our nation's ability to wage war. It would be a bold national leader who, confronted by the uncertainties, ambiguities and discontinuities of the contemporary strategic situation, dismissed the ability to wage war as a thing of the past.

Why? Because as Clausewitz famously prescribed, military ability is intrinsic to the nature and purpose of the state. The ability to leverage military power to safeguard the citizens is embedded in the very concept of the modern state. Thus, the Navy is truly a national enterprise.

The constant that underpins the state's ability to continue policy by other means is the armed force available to it and its willingness to use that force. Deterrence, and for that matter, sea control, power projection and naval presence are all consequences of the state's ability to deliver strategic lethality, either alone or in coalition with like-minded states. And as a fifth generation navy, the RAN needs the requisite lethality to meet the nation's objectives now and into the future

The Defence White Paper, released by government in February 2016, has set the Navy on a new course. Not only has government redefined the Navy as a system rather than a collection of cobbled-together plat-forms but, more importantly, it has also repositioned the Navy as a national enterprise. The announcement that Australia would partner with DCNS to design and build twelve submarines under a rolling build program confirms our nation's long-term intention.

This represents a fundamental transformation in thinking about what the Navy actually is, where it fits in our national architecture and how it relates to the national economic infrastructure. In short, the Navy and the substantial re-equipment program that government has decided upon sits squarely within government's innovation agenda. From the stump-jump plough to Wi-Fi, Australians have a great track record as inventors. Innovation, however, goes beyond discovery to encompass new ways of doing things, of integrating invention into the way we conceive and design our national enterprise. And this is nowhere more evident than in the way that government envisages Navy's role in a new approach to manufacturing and industry.

At the heart of Navy's transition from a consumer of industrial output to a partner in high-tech manufacturing are the continuous and rolling shipbuilding programs, whereby industry and the Navy combine to deliver a more efficient and more effective maritime defence system. Partnership, of course, depends critically on trust, and that is what the Navy is absolutely intent upon building as we move to a new way of delivering defence capabilities.

It is disappointing to find some commentators representing our new shipbuilding program as a kind of salvage operation for Australia's manufacturing industry. This shipbuilding policy extends far beyond the construction of hulls in Australian yards to the design and development of the systems that fill those hulls. This is a program aimed at the entire Australian manufacturing sector, particularly those areas where invention, design and development combine to deliver innovation nationally. Every state and territory will necessarily be involved.

With just under fifty government-owned and operated ships and twelve future submarines in the national inventory, government is confident that there is a sustainable work program that the national engineering, systems design and integration, construction and management capabilities, folded into a continuous shipbuilding program, are able to meet indefinitely. So, too, is the RAN.

The historical stop-start approach to warship acquisition, with its high start-up and termination costs, is only part of the problem. The more acute problem has been the lack of ambition and imagination to maintain the impetus that transforms Australia from a ship purchaser to a ship producer. If England, France, Spain and Sweden could initiate and sustain such a transformation in the sixteenth century, there is no reason that Australia cannot do so in the twenty-first century.

To realise its ambition to reposition the Navy as a national enterprise, government is focusing on three core inputs that must underpin a continuous shipbuilding approach to sustaining and continually transforming naval war-fighting capabilities.

First, education and skills development are paramount. Our universities, TAFEs and research organisations play an essential role in providing the professional and technical skills without which there is no industry. Whether it is naval architecture, propulsion design, sensor and weapons design and engineering or organisational design, industry demands advanced skills.

Second, workforce design and flexibility are also critical. As was mentioned earlier, the Navy is already planning for greater flexibility in career management and greater integration between the Service and civilian components of its workforce. Similarly, industry will need to leverage the skills, especially in engineering, that the Navy already has while complementing those skills from within the industry base. This will demand innovative approaches to workforce management, generating new and exciting opportunities for young professionals and technicians to work across a number of institutional frameworks.

Third, investment is the essential driver of national enterprise. Here, our investment institutions will need to develop new ways of planning and managing the long-term capital investments without which a continuous shipbuilding program will be unachievable. This will require innovative and imaginative ways of partnering with foreign direct investors to ensure both satisfactory returns on investment and the capability outcomes that are the fundamental reason for continuous shipbuilding, and the ongoing evolution of ships. For the Navy to be able to address the strategic uncertainties and complexities that are progressively characterising the twenty-first century, we need a new way of doing business. It is no longer sensible or even possible for Australia to pick and choose among individual elements of our national industrial capacity as though naval capability development was some kind of smorgasbord.

What government is intent upon creating is a fully integrated approach to naval capability planning, development, delivery and sustainment. While the Offshore Patrol Vessels, the new generation frigates, the Air Warfare Destroyers and, of course, our future submarines will provide a significant industrial challenge, it is a challenge that the Navy is confident that it can meet in partnership with industry. It is not that industry leverages the Navy, or vice versa. Rather, continuous shipbuilding provides us with the critical tool to build and maintain a strategic maritime capability over the long term. This is what is meant, in part at least, by 'Navy as a national enterprise'.

Availability and sustainment[38]

The RAN can have the best weapons systems in the world, but they are useless if they cannot leave the wharf. Deterrence can have effect only if our ships can sail; if our submarines can dive; and if our aircraft can fly. And, if our assets can be repaired and replaced. This, of course, is a major reason why continuous shipbuilding makes such great sense. In the event hostilities break out after deterrence has failed, our nation will be able to reinstate lost capability. Without forces available for tasking, government cannot fulfil its global objectives; it cannot contribute; it cannot deter; and it definitely cannot defend.

It is the role of a Chief of Navy to ensure that strategic purpose, operational concepts, and capability requirements are designed into our ships and aircraft. And it is equally important to recognise that lethality depends on the way we sustain our maritime capabilities. This is of fundamental importance. The efficacy of our sustainment arrangements is essential to our ability to generate both force availability (the ability to be at sea—seaworthiness) and capability (the ability to achieve assigned missions—battleworthiness).

The availability of our future fleet will depend on a new enterprise approach to acquisition and sustainment that Navy, the Capability Acquisition and Support Group, and industry will need to develop and maintain. Of course, robust sustainment arrangements need to be complemented by the reliability and robustness of our deployed systems in the first instance. This points to the fact that we must build sustainment into both the design and operation of our fleet. If there is a criticism of the rhetoric of the past few decades, it is that it focused too much on theoretical capability without due recognition of the capabilities actually available, and without full recognition of the need for complex sustainment to maintain ongoing availability.

The obvious question is 'how?' How do we ensure that we can manage our assets to deliver to government the forces necessary for our national security? There is no single answer. But it is important to recognise that there is a growing appreciation within Defence that different capabilities need to be managed in different ways to ensure success. Moreover, there is a growing appreciation that the effectiveness of the entire system cannot depend on any single point of capability failure.

Sailors everywhere know the importance of the adage 'don't spoil the ship for a ha'penny's worth of tar'. This may sound like another 'blinding glimpse of the obvious', but over previous decades the wish to stretch out the value of the defence dollar meant that financial parsimony left the Navy under-equipped and under-manned. That is why we have been subject to review after review over the last thirty years. Government has resolved to fix this problem by instituting a program of continuous shipbuilding that will deliver both the number of platforms that Navy needs to be able to meet the tasks set for it by government and the capabilities those platforms need to constitute the naval system.

Determining the numbers

There are three questions that are central to defence capability planning. First, what must the Defence Force be able to do? Second, what are the capabilities necessary to achieve government objectives? And third, how many platforms are needed to deploy those capabilities? This is not a hit or miss issue. An enormous amount of Defence's analytical effort goes into addressing those three questions, and the answers are based on extensive consideration of the various issues that combine to make force definition and source selection such truly 'wicked' problems.

To judge by some of the commentary that has attended major government acquisition announcements in recent years, the elements that determine numbers are not well understood, even among informed commentators. So a brief run-down of the factors that ultimately determine 'what' and 'how many' might help those who are interested in 'why this number submarines' and 'why a continuous ship building program in Australia'.

Chiefs of Navy must be able to advise government on the following key factors in determining what kinds of vessels the Navy needs and how many provide the essential (and basic) capability.

First, where does government want the Navy to operate? This is perhaps the fundamental question, since it is driven by long-term strategic considerations. While it is clear that the Navy must be able to operate in the direct defence of Australia in the maritime approaches, it is essential that the Navy is able to take the conflict up to the adversary itself. As mentioned earlier, the conduct of operations in armed conflict comprehends both the defensive and offensive dynamics of war. And since submarines are essentially offensive systems, the Navy must be able to operate them at a considerable distance from Australia.

Australia is extraordinarily fortunate in its geographical position, since any armed threat has to cover great distances to reach us. Equally, when threats do emerge, we must be able to cover great distances to deal with them. Accordingly, we need to be able to ensure that government has the ability to deploy offensive capabilities as far away as the northern Pacific and the western Indian Ocean. Typically, submarines are at sea for extended periods. But, given the long transit times, the actual time that a submarine is available for offensive operations is less than the period of deployment. This means, in order to sustain a vessel on station, other vessels will be in transit to and from an operational area.

Second, for how long does government want the strategic strike capability of the submarine to be on station? This is the 'killer' question that really drives numbers. To keep one submarine on station continuously requires a number of vessels, especially since a crew must be fully rested after duty at sea, where there are no holidays, no weekends off, no opportunities for outdoors recreation, but only the reality of six hours on/six hours off. Nor can submarines be rotated indefinitely: the sea is a harsh and punishing environment, exacting a heavy toll on both people and equipment. So submarines have to be berthed for maintenance and servicing.

Third, how many stations might government want the submarines to tend? This is where the going gets really tough, because for each station where a submarine is required, the pressure on the submarine force begins to grow. To keep submarines on continuous station in a number of places actually requires a number of supporting vessels, because the pressures on training and maintenance, crew rotation and personnel replacement (our sailors cannot stay at sea indefinitely) are inexorable.

Fourth, the deep maintenance demands on the submarine force mean that a major refit is required every decade if the vessels are to sustain a meaningful contribution. A refit ensures the vessels remain both seaworthy and battle-worthy and, consequently, refitting ensures the crew is placed at least risk.

Fifth, the training demands on the submarine force are extremely oner-ous. Many of the skills (for instance, escaping from a submerged vessel that is damaged) are found nowhere else in the Navy. So submarines need to be available for training as well as for the conduct of offensive operations.

All of this is further compounded by systems obsolescence, the intro-duction of new and improved systems, changes in allied and coalition combined operating systems (which need to be practised in joint and com-bined exercises) and a range of other operating complexities that impact on both availability and sustainability—and, of course, there is affordability.

Consideration of these and other factors led successive governments to establish twelve as the essential submarine capability. The next issue is: how to acquire and maintain that capability over time. And that is what persuaded government to identify a continuous rolling program as the best way both to deliver the capability in a sustainable way and to manage continuous improvement as the capability matures into the future. This approach has set us on the course of a great national endeavour—an invest-ment in the future of the Navy and the nation.

Continuous shipbuilding: Implications for innovation

Continuous shipbuilding is how the nation can ensure its naval vessels are acquired and sustained to guarantee preparedness. It is about building evolu-tion and continuous improvement into availability. Continuous shipbuilding also provides certainty for industry—not just for the life of one project, but for sustained capability into the future. It is an initiative of national significance.

The Defence organisation as a whole is currently examining ways to reduce the skills loss across the shipbuilding workforce and mitigate the effects of a 'cold re-start' after the completion of the current three-ship Destroyer program. This is a significant strategic initiative for both the Navy and the nation. But to deliver on the plan of government, we need to design a totally new way of doing business.

To this end, a number of specialist commentators have drawn attention to the success of the ANZAC project, and have suggested that we need to replicate that project. It was a project that promised a general-purpose frigate, and it delivered a general-purpose frigate. In some ways, replicating this project has merit. But in drawing on the various features that made the ANZAC project successful, we need to appreciate that it was a freestanding project with a beginning and certainly with an end. It started, then it stopped.

Continuous shipbuilding will place naval construction in the sinews of national industrial capacity, giving real and continuing meaning to Navy as a national enterprise. It is an opportunity for government, Defence, Navy and industry, working together, to cement the foundations of capability across the economy, thereby creating an industrial inheritance for future generations of Australians.

The role of industry

Chiefs of Navy are responsible through the Chief of the Defence Force to the government of the day for providing trained, mission-ready vessels. That means the ships, submarines and aircraft in the fleet must be available as planned: their maintenance and sustainment must be conducted predictably, reliably, on time, and on budget. Consequently, the Navy needs partners in industry that will not only deliver the required levels of readiness but will also translate cost effectiveness into enhanced readiness. To deliver this outcome, industry needs to understand the importance of optimising the readiness of the current systems and capturing and managing the required skill sets and knowledge base. Industry needs to bring to the national naval enterprise the latest in effective techniques to improve affordability, such as Total Asset Management.

This does not imply any criticism of industry. Navy sees industry as a valued partner and as a central part of the modern naval enterprise. It is only by fully appreciating this enterprise approach that we will capture the opportunities generated by this ambitious program. In supporting this outcome, industry needs to understand the technology growth paths and the long-term implications of systems and technology providing operational availability at an affordable cost.

This is a crucial observation, because continuous shipbuilding is not just about the first ship to roll off the production line. Rather, it is about the one after the one after next—the replacement for the future frigate, the growth path of the new submarines, subsequent generations of the Air Warfare Destroyer. It is about innovation. It is about continuous improvement. It is about Navy and the nation. Continuous shipbuilding recognises that we truly understand the synergistic nature of systems on ships and how they impact on our planning for sustainment and availability. Some of these systems can be expected to last the life of the asset. Others will need to be updated several times throughout the life of the platform. At the outset of design, industry and Navy will together need to be aligned with this concept.

Benefits of a continuous build program

In addition to maintaining and developing industry over the long term, we should highlight the important role that the continuous build program plays in supporting the delivery of innovation into the national naval enterprise. Innovation is an oft-used and frequently misapplied word. In the case of continuous shipbuilding, innovation will be a critical feature. Continuous building is a remarkable and dramatic leap ahead; it promises opportunity, and demands a new way of thinking and a new way of doing business.

One of the greatest opportunities that continuous shipbuilding provides is the ability to look at analysis, design, construction and sustainment collectively, or, as it might be better described: thinking, designing and doing, not as a series of sequential activities, but as concurrent activities. Synergy and synchronicity come together.

Accordingly, these features will provide the environment for innovation to thrive in the naval fleet system. Continuous shipbuilding offers many cost-effective opportunities to be innovative in the way we build and sustain the fleet. However, it is important to be realistic about what we are attempting to do. We cannot disconnect from the fact that we will inevitably begin with a mature design. Where we take benefit is in managing the system that supports that design—data recording, real time maintenance management, capability and systems evolution, the exploitation of disruptive technologies. This is essentially about availability. Looking beyond the build, we must design for sustainment.

Hence we need to take advantage of new technologies and systems, whether they are domestic or from the global market so that they can be integrated into both the build and sustainment activities. Doing so will enable the continuous building plan to evolve because, while the program will be enduring, the technology will advance.

This is what a twenty-first-century naval enterprise is all about: networked collaboration. The continuous build program will not only change the way that business cases are developed, it will also change the way that business is done. Industry must be attuned to this and grasp its implications for the investment decisions that government will make regarding both technology and people.

THE NAVY AND THE COMMUNITY

IT HAS PROBABLY become clear by now that the Navy is a critical part of the Australian community: the community is where our people are born, bred and educated; the community is where we live and work; the community is where all of us who have been in the Navy continue to contribute to our national strength and well-being when we depart from the Navy; the community is what sustains us in peace and war; and, most importantly, it is the community that all of us in the Navy are prepared to sacrifice our lives to defend. The Navy, along with the Army and the Air Force, are uniformed and disciplined Services, as are the police and other first response organisations that support public order, personal safety and community well-being. We are all volunteer Services, and that goes to the heart of the compact between us and the community we come from and serve. We are the community, and the community is us. We should always remember the fundamental truth of the remarks made by the Australian Prime Minister at the interment in 1993 of the Unknown Soldier in the Hall of Remembrance at the Australian War Memorial. Referring specifically to the 100,000 Australians who died in the wars of the twentieth century, Prime Minister Keating said: 'He is all of them. And he is one of us'.

This is not just some pious or sentimental statement of what it might be like in an ideal world. It is a statement of fact, founded in our creation as a nation in 1901, which sits at the centre of our democracy. Our democracy is built upon the fundamental freedoms we all enjoy—freedoms based on shared values as expressed in the term 'rule of law'. And right at the core of our democracy is the determination to defend those freedoms should they come under threat or attack.

It is for this reason that the community turns to the ADF to defend the nation against armed aggression, and incidentally pays for it. And, as part of the ADF, the Navy conducts our national defence not only in proximate waters but also in distant waters where an aggressor may be much more vulnerable to attack. At all times, however, the Navy depends on its deep links with the Australian community. Our people—officers, non-commissioned officers and enlisted sailors—come from all parts of Australia. Many people who join the Navy come from regional and rural Australia, and maintain deep links with their communities. All around Australia, there is a strong sense of pride and a powerful sense of belonging exhibited by both the families and communities that our recruits come from and by the recruits themselves. This pride and belonging is deeply mutual.

The Navy is a profession, built around core values, an ethos of service, and strong traditions. In common with all the other professions, we have a strong sense of identity, pride in our history, respect for our common purpose and, above all, powerful interpersonal bonds best reflected in the duty of care we have for each other. To maintain our professionalism, we draw on every talent and skill the community has to offer. We rely on the community to provide the pool of outstanding recruits we continually attract. Equally, the community relies on the Navy to nurture, protect and train that talent, so that the women and men who make up the Navy can eventually return to their families and communities all the better for having served. This is why Chiefs of Navy place such an emphasis on the need for all the Navy's leaders, particularly those in our training establishments, to pay the closest attention to the physical and moral well-being of our young sailors and midshipmen. Parents and families pay us an extraordinary honour in entrusting their children to us, an honour that we wish to repay to the maximum extent.

In a world of accelerating strategic challenge and technological complexity, the Navy is constantly on the lookout for more and better professional skills within the Service. This is something that the community both understands and supports. The skills, aptitude and willingness to learn that our young sailors and midshipmen display is of the highest order. The Navy is its people—all its people.

In the last forty years, the RAN has changed enormously, and for the better. Traditionally, the Navy has been a particularly masculine profession, with women recruits allocated mainly to shore-based support functions. Largely as a result of recruitment and staffing changes set in train by Vice Admiral Ian MacDougall in the early nineties, women have moved progressively into the full range of naval warfare and specialist categories. Women serve in the most senior ranks of the Navy. Women currently serve in our submarines, in our destroyers, frigates, patrol vessels and other surface ships, in the Fleet Air Arm and across all shore-based specialties. Women have commanded our ships and shore establishments. At present, some thirty percent of the cadets at the Australian Defence Force Academy are women, a percentage that will grow further. The leadership of the RAN is deeply committed to gender equity and equality, as we are to honouring the right of all our personnel to their sexual orientation and gender preference. The mores of the Navy are the mores of the community, and that is as it should be.

Embedded as the Navy is in the Australian community, there are key ideas that guide our approach to managing the naval workforce: leadership, responsibility, trust. Every person in the Navy is expected to lead, to set an example of high principle and conscientiousness. People are expected to be responsible. They are trusted to be dependable and they are relied upon to bear the whole burden of their obligations. More than the technological challenges of highly specialised jobs, these ideas give service in the Navy a deep sense of purpose, meaning and reward. The right person for the job will not just be technically smart. The right person will lead by example, living up to those values that define the Australian nation. The right people enable and inspire other people to play their part.

This is an essential feature of Navy's leadership model. To perform its duties and meet its objectives, the Navy can only operate as a 'team of teams'. There is no place for the heroic individualist, the solipsist or the soloist. Rather, the Navy's leaders must empower their team members to perform to the best of their individual abilities and generate the cohesion in the team that, in turn, allows the Navy to operate as a system. This is a big ask. But it is what government expects of the Navy. It is also a key accountability of any Chief of Navy.

Andrew Gordon's book, *The Rules of the Game,* has been mentioned a number of times in the course of this essay, so one final mention will not go astray. His discussion of leadership and command in the light of the Battle of Jutland is permeated by whimsy and disdain, in equal measure. His twenty-fifth 'blinding glimpse of the obvious' reads:

> It is sobering to reflect that, in order to get into a position where his higher-command abilities become an issue, *Every proven military incompetent has previously displayed attributes which his superiors rewarded.*[39]

Modern naval leadership is not about ticking boxes, mouthing doctrinal platitudes or managing upwards. It is about imagination, ingenuity, professionalism, empowerment and, most importantly, the devolution of responsibility. To become the leaders of the future, young officers need to be given their heads if they are to display tactical and operational initiative. This is where resilience comes from in the broader Australian community, and it is certainly where resilience comes from in the Navy. We talk a lot about flexibility and agility, but flexible and agile command is a product of practice, not the number of thick gold bands on the bottom of the sleeve or the number of stars on the shoulder boards.

The Navy is, of course, more than a profession. It is a career. But whereas in the past, the naval career has been continuous and unbroken, community expectations—both current and prospective—suggest that the twenty-first-century naval career may be a procession of naval appointments interleaved with experience garnered in other occupations. Among the many ways we need to think more innovatively, the Navy needs to make it easier for people to 'come and go'. In some ways, the RAN is already familiar with movements into and out of the Service as naval reserve officers perform duties for a period then revert to civilian life. For example, medical specialists and lawyers currently practise in both the Navy and in private practice, to the benefit of both the Navy and the community. The service of reservists offers an important bridge to the civil community and the Navy. Other ways we can foster connection between the Navy and the community might be in the placement of Navy people in universities, in the same way that we offer technical sailors the opportunity for industry out-placements. Beyond the human connection, opportunities such as these raise awareness and technical skill. We are already witnessing the growth of multi-skilling in the modern workforce as new technologies and new opportunities combine to create new jobs. The application of high levels of manual labour in industry, for instance, has already given way to robotics, and in advanced manufacturing workers are just as likely to have skills in computing to complement trade skills.

Earlier, this essay addressed the importance of the 'human dimension' in operating the Navy as a system, and the need for the Navy to accommodate the career and lifestyle choices of its members. We must devise better systems for welcoming back into the Navy those who, for one reason or another, have a need to separate at some point during their careers. This is not simply to maximise the return on investment associated with training and professional development. Rather, it recognises that broader experience generates broader skills. Time out is not time wasted. To achieve this, however, Navy's culture will need to continue evolving in line with changes in the attitudes and practices of the Australian community as a whole. Just as we need to be agile and flexible in the conduct of operations, we need to be agile and flexible as an organisation. Mindsets that might have suited a more predictable past are not often of much use in dealing with an uncertain future. Adaptability needs to be hard-wired into both our leadership and our organisation.

THE NAVY AND THE NATION

I T IS THE privilege of Chiefs of Navy to rub shoulders with leaders from all walks of life: industry, commerce, banking, financial services, agriculture, mining, academia, the media, the public service, politics, the religions, sport, the arts, and virtually every other field of endeavour in Australia. What impresses the most is the enormous and shared sense of involvement and investment that these leaders have in the great national enterprise we call Australia. The sense of optimism and common purpose at the national level is something that transcends the usual competition between intra- and inter-sectoral players, between the states, between the banks, between the universities, between the miners, and between our political parties. This is exactly the kind of nation that is worth defending.

The ADF is the only organisation in Australia that is mandated to employ lethal force against those external actors who would seek to attack or otherwise constrain us. As such, the ADF employs focused and deliberate power to guarantee the nation's security against armed aggression. And in this task, the Navy plays the central role of both protecting the seaborne trade on which we depend for our livelihoods and well-being, at the same time taking the fight up to would-be aggressors, either through deterrence or the decisive lethality around which the Navy's systems are built.

A nation's strength ultimately depends on the strength of its institutions—economic, legal, justice, administrative, social, cultural, political and religious. Much of the strategic uncertainly that characterises this century is a consequence of the political instability, economic inequality, social disadvantage and religious division that are the direct result of weak or broken national institutions. And the nations that generate the greatest strategic concern are those where corruption, political nepotism, kleptocracy, criminal conspiracy, dysfunctional courts, controls on free speech and a cowed population combine to define a broken nation. Fortunately, Australia boasts strong foundations. Our society is not corrupt, and where criminality does occur, our justice institutions investigate, prosecute and punish.

The Navy is proud to be a strong national institution, displaying characteristics in common with our other major institutions. We value our reputation, and the high standards on which that reputation rests. We value the character of our people, for this is a strength of character that makes our institutions robust and enduring. To paraphrase Deakin, it is the individual character of our citizens that ultimately makes our nation strong and enduring.

The Navy is also a significant national employer. We do much more than give people a job, however. The Navy both attracts skills and educates people, with an enormous emphasis on personal development. We take recruits and turn them into leaders—leaders who enrich both the Navy and the community at large. Naval personnel of all ranks participate in community associations, and upon leaving the Navy at the end of their careers, many naval personnel take up new positions as community leaders, corporate leaders, heads of not-for-profit and other charitable organisations, and even as governors of states. As an employer, the Navy operates within the full suite of national skill sets, contributing to the national knowledge base in a manner that both enables and strengthens the national industry capacity. This is why the continuous shipbuilding program mandated by government makes such sense: Navy is already there.

In a very important sense, the Navy serves as a custodian of our national values and national identity. This is a role we share with many other groups. Our indigenous peoples are the custodians of the land on which we live. Our various religious bodies are the custodians of different religious faiths. Our parliaments and courts are the custodians of our freedom and the 'rule of law'.

Our schools and universities are the custodians of learning and knowledge. Our community groups and volunteer associations are the custodians of the resilience without which we would find it difficult to recover from natural disasters. But when we attend the Anzac Day parades around Australia, and when we observe our forces operating abroad, we cannot but appreciate the extent to which our Armed Services give expression to important aspects of our national identity—perseverance, endurance, loyalty, bravery and a deep compassion for our fellow human beings. With the Army and the Air Force, the Navy is proud of the place it occupies in maintaining the sense of national 'self' that identifies us as Australians, irrespective of our race, religion or social status.

So it is that the Navy takes particular pride in its role as a clear and very identifiable representative of Australia and what it stands for. This is not simply pride in the white ensign, though we are certainly proud of that. Rather, it is pride in what the white ensign stands for—the nation as a whole. Whether on patrol in the Arabian Sea, operating in the waters of South-East Asia, providing assistance to our friends in the Pacific, our ships and their companies extend our national influence while contributing to security on the high seas. Our naval personnel all round the world, whether in our embassies, foreign naval colleges, or negotiating capability developments with international equipment suppliers, display all the qualities that make them individually Australian—professionalism, generosity, good humour, a sense of the ridiculous, and a great ability to laugh at themselves. Navy also performs that other important role in a lively democracy: we represent ourselves to ourselves. While, as a nation, we do not set much store by icons or any form of jingoistic excess, we nonetheless look to a few symbols that serve to remind us of who we are. Our sporting teams and top athletes capture that strong image of national performance, as do our cultural identities—musicians, actors, writers, dancers, film-makers and scientists—who hold up a mirror to ourselves, at the same time showing the world who we are and the pride we have in that. The people who make up our Navy do that, too, perhaps less noticeably but no less effectively. And Chiefs of Navy, who have the privilege of meeting a great many Australians, are constantly humbled by the respect they show to them, not for who they are but for what they represent—the Navy.

In concluding this essay, it is important once again to touch on the continuity that has been such a remarkable feature of Australia's development from a fledgling community of fewer than four million people at Federation to the thriving nation of over twenty-four million in 2016. Our great-grandparents would be proud to see what their children and their successors have achieved in realising their hopes and ambitions for this great continent. Underpinning this continuity are the fundamental principles of law, democratic politics, public administration and strategy that, in combination, deliver the framework within which economic prosperity and social harmony can develop. And central to this is our ability to manage our connectivity with the world, to defend our interests when we need to, and to contribute to the efforts of like-minded nations to act in the common good. The ANZAC experience so early in our history as a nation set the tone for our military tradition and played into the establishment of our national identity.

The Navy and the Nation is the title of this essay. But, as was acknowledged earlier, it is a title that has been used before. In June 1903, speaking at a meeting of the Fitzroy branch of the Australian Natives Association (of which, incidentally, Alfred Deakin was a member), the Governor of Victoria spoke in terms that, their stilted cadences notwithstanding, echo Mahan and resonate over a century later. That he was by profession a British Army engineer perhaps lends greater weight to his views! His address was entitled 'The Navy and the Nation':

> It could safely be asserted that the empire depended absolutely upon the seaborne commerce, in which directly or indirectly every citizen was interested; that the loss of this commerce as a result of being overpowered on the seas would bring ruin and disruption, and that the guardianship of our means of existence and our hope of the future depended wholly upon the efficiency and sufficiency of His Majesty's Navy. Australians, who lived secure in this southern ocean, and were much engrossed in their local problems, might easily come to forget the force to which they owed alike their territorial integrity, their progress and their prospects of future development.[40]

The fact is that Australians did not forget the realities of their strategic position or the implications of their long-term strategic interests. The Navy is inseparable from the nation.

ACKNOWLEDGEMENTS

THAT THIS ESSAY has seen the light of day is a tribute to the persistence, indeed insistence, of my recent Chief of Staff, Commodore Tim Brown RAN. His constant refrain 'Well, if that is the case, why do you not tell everyone' finally overcame my usual reticence, not to mention my appreciation of the need for a sustained narrative on the purpose of naval service and career. The day-to-day demands on a chief of service are as onerous as they are inexorable. So to produce this essay, I have relied on the intellectual and research capacities of Lieutenant Commander Richard Adams RAN, whose ability to discover entertaining but completely pertinent technical references is second to none.

Ideas are what lend authority and credibility to leadership. I am indebted to my two deputies, Rear Admirals Michael Van Balen RAN (ret'd) and Michael Noonan RAN, for their constant conversation, discussion and deeply informed comment. I am also very grateful to my former Chief of Staff, Commodore James McCormack RAN, for his constant provision of new and interesting ideas.

I have also enjoyed the constructive and insightful inputs from Mr Marc Ablong, in the Department of Defence. Finally, this is an essay to which many pens have made a contribution, and its continuity of argument and consistency of style are largely due to the advice and editorial skills of Mr Allan Behm, a former head of the International Policy and Strategy Divisions in the Department of Defence.

Many people have worked on this essay, in research and offering editorial adjustment. I am grateful for their collaboration and contribution. But the buck stops with me. As Chief of Navy I put my name to this text as the narrative for the Navy today and for tomorrow.

However, though I offer my ideas as Chief of Navy, they are not necessarily the views of the government of Australia or the Department of Defence. Any errors or omissions are mine.

NOTES

1 'Time spent on reconnaissance is seldom wasted.' Often attributed to Field Marshal Rommel, who was quoted wonderfully by Admiral Sandy Woodward in *One Hundred Days: The Memoirs of the Falkland Battle Group Commander* (Great Britain: HarperCollins, 1992), p. 86.

2 David Stevens and John Reeve (eds), *The Navy and the Nation* (Sydney: Allen & Unwin, 2005).

3 Geoffrey Till, *Seapower: A Guide for the Twenty-first Century* (London: Frank Cass, 2004), p. 31.

4 In his subsequent 1975 text, *Death of the Lucky Country*, Donald Horne offered an interesting insight. He wrote: 'When I invented the phrase ['the lucky country'] in 1964 to describe Australia … I had in mind the idea of Australia as a derived society whose prosperity in the great age of manufacturing came mainly from the luck of its historical origins. It was sufficiently like the innovative industrial societies of the west to prosper from their innovations; it didn't have to think up much in the way of techniques of design or organization in manufacturing for itself'.

5 David Stevens, '1901–1913: The Genesis of the Australian Navy,' in D. Stevens (ed.), *The Royal Australian Navy* (Oxford University Press: Melbourne, 2001), pp. 11–13. Stevens describes how the Royal Australian Navy grew from the separate colonial navies, which were amalgamated and transferred to Commonwealth control on Federation, and notes that, in 1901 the absence of legislated administrative controls meant that colonial naval forces remained under the

authority of state naval commandants. G.L. Macandie, *The Genesis of the Royal Australian Navy* (Sydney: Alfred Henry Pettifer, Government Printer, 1949), p. 207. Macandie records that it was the Commonwealth *Defence Act* (1904), which facilitated the appointment by Prime Minister Reid of Captain W.R. Creswell as Commonwealth Director of Naval Forces. Creswell sat on the Board of Naval Administration constituted by the Minister for Defence (J.W. McCay, as President) and Mr J.A. Thompson (Finance Member). The *Naval Defence Act* (1910) made for an enlarged Naval Board.

6 David Cannadine, *Ornamentalism: How the British Saw their Empire* (London: Penguin, 2002), p. 39.

7 It should be noted that the global reach of the RN reflected the span of British commercial interests. See Robert Massie, *Dreadnought: Britain, Germany and the Coming of the Great War* (London: Pimlico, 1994), pp. xxi–xxv, and p. 434.

8 Prime Minister Alfred Deakin, *HoR Hansard*, No. 50, 1907, Friday 13 December 1907, p. 7510.

9 Franklin D. Roosevelt *FDR: Selected Speeches of President Franklin D. Roosevelt* (Florida: Red and Black Publishers, 2020), p. 145. The text of the Four Freedoms Speech, as it is now known, can be found at http://www.fdrlibrary.marist.edu/pdfs/fftext.pdf (accessed on 8 May 2016).

10 Chief of the Defence Force Admiral Chris Barrie, *The Australian Approach to Warfare* (Canberra: 2002), p. 1.

11 Carl von Clausewitz, *On War* (trans. Michael Howard and Peter Paret) (Princeton, 1984), p. 370.

12 This mordant but accurate observation is quoted by Norman Friedman, *Fighting the Great War at Sea: Strategy, Tactic and Technology* (Annapolis: Naval Institute Press, 2014), p. 172.

13 In his book, *Engage the Enemy More Closely* (London, Sydney, Auckland, Toronto: Hodder & Stoughton, 1991) the historian Corelli Barnett notes (p. 5) that the High Seas Fleet sank 111,980 tons of British warships. The Grand Fleet sank 62,233 tons of German ships. The Royal Navy suffered loss in the order of 6250 lives; the High Seas Fleet lost 2500 people.

14 Sir John Keegan in *The Price of Admiralty* (London: Hutchinson, 1988), p. 180, cites Ernle Chatfield, who was serving as Flag Captain aboard Beatty's flagship *Lion* as follows: 'What would happen (in Nelson's time) when two ships met and engaged was, as far as materiel was concerned, known within definite limits from handed-down experience and from a hundred sea-fights. Nelson knew exactly the risks he ran and accurately allowed for them. He had clear knowledge from long-considered fighting experiences how long his ships could endure the temporary gunnery disadvantage necessary in order to gain the dominant tactical position he aimed ... for ... we had to buy that experience for our

weapons were untried. The risks could not be measured without that experience … [Before Jutland] Dreadnoughts had never engaged, [and] modern massed destroyer attack had never taken place'.

15 Andrew Gordon, *The Rules of the Game: Jutland and British Naval Command* (London: John Murray: 2005), p. 582. Gordon observes this 'to be especially important in [times] of technical change, for it is then that specialists get further ahead of general knowledge'.

16 This is, perhaps, the most penetrating and powerful of the many insights that Carl von Clausewitz brings to the modern understanding of the nature of war. While often quoted, it is even more often misunderstood. Explaining his concept, Clausewitz wrote: 'War is not a mere act of policy but a true political instrument, a continuation of political activity by other means. What remains peculiar to war is simply the peculiar nature of its means. War in general, and the commander in any specific instance, is entitled to require that the trend and designs of policy shall not be inconsistent with these means. That, of course, is no small demand; but however much it may affect political aims in a given case, it will never do more than modify them. The political object is the goal, war is the means of reaching it, and means can never be considered in isolation from their purpose'. *On War*, p. 87.

17 Churchill's radio broadcast, 'Report on the War', 27 April 1941.

18 'Doctrine' describes the shared, professional understanding, which is important in military life. In *The Rules of the Game*, Andrew Gordon describes ambient doctrine, the inexplicit sense of ideas that texture the fabric of military culture (Gordon, *op. cit.*, p. 580). But doctrine can equally be written, as a formal statement for reference. This is the way the word is used here. We would not contemplate resurrecting the tactical doctrines on which Nelson based his victories.

19 Till, *op. cit.*, p. 155. See also: Vice Admiral Stansfield Turner, 'Missions of the US Navy', *Naval War College Review* (March–April 1974), p. 5. 'Today, the balance of naval resources and attention devoted to … Strategic Deterrence, Sea Control, Projection of Power Ashore, and Naval Presence, is especially difficult because of their complex interdependence and because almost all naval forces have multimission capabilities.'

20 See Turner, *op. cit.*, p. 5.

21 Sir Walter Ralegh, 'A Discourse of the Invention of Ships, Anchors, Compass, &c.', *The Works of Sir Walter Ralegh, Kt.*, vol. 8, p. 325 (1829, reprinted 1965).

22 A. T. Mahan, *The Influence of Sea Power upon History 1660–1783* (London, 1890), p. 138. Chapter 1, which deals with the elements of sea power, remains a powerful and persuasive account of naval power as it relates to the power of the nation, and is worth reading in its own right.

23 Till, *op. cit.*, p. 41.

24 For a totally fascinating account of how Europe stumbled into the cataclysm of World War I, see Christopher Clark, *The Sleepwalkers: How Europe went to War in 1914* (New York: HarperCollins, 2014).

25 See Philip Bobbitt, *The Shield of Achilles* (London: Penguin, 2002), pp. 69–74 and elsewhere.

26 See Sir Ernest Satow, *A Guide to Diplomatic Practice* (London: Longmans, Green & Co., 1958), p. 1.

27 W. S. Churchill, *The World Crisis*, vol. 1, 1911–1914 (Toronto: Macmillan, 1923), p. 45.

28 Bobbitt, *op. cit.*, p. 813.

29 Turner, *op cit.*, p. 39.

30 Quoted from A.W. Jose, *The Royal Australian Navy* (Brisbane, 1987 reprint of 1928 edition), p. lviii, by David Stevens 'The Great White Fleet's 1908 Visit to Australia' at http://www.navy.gov.au/history/feature-histories/great-white-fleet%E2%80%99s-1908-visit-australia (accessed on 7 June 2016).

31 Found at http://www.navy.gov.au/history/feature-histories/great-white-fleet's-1908-visit-australia (accessed on 21 June 2016).

32 Till, *op. cit.*, p. 31.

33 See the interesting essay by Sir Tipene O'Regan, a leader of the Ngāi Tahu *iwi*, 'The Dimension of Kinship' in A. Grimes, L. Wevers and G. Sullivan, *States of Mind* (Wellington: Institute of Policy Studies, 2002), pp. 35–8.

34 See von Clausewitz, *op. cit.*, p. 101.

35 Gordon E. Moore, 'Cramming More Components onto Integrated Circuits', *Electronics*, vol. 38, no. 8, 19 April 1965, pp. 114–17.

36 See Annie Sneed, *Scientific American*, 19 May 2015 at http://www.scientificamerican.com/article/moore-s-law-keeps-going-defying-expectations/ (accessed on 29 May 2016).

37 Till, *op. cit.*, p. 141.

38 In *Working and Thinking on the Waterfront* (New York: Harper & Row, 1969), Eric Hoffer wrote: 'It is the capacity for maintenance which is the best test for the vigor and stamina of a society. Any society can be galvanized for a while, to building something, but the will and the skill to keep things in good repair day-in and day-out are fairly rare'. Hoffer is cited by the National Research Council of the National Academies in their report, *Intelligent Sustainment and Renewal of Department of Energy Facilities and Infrastructure* (Washington, DC: National Academies Press, 2004), p. 29.

39 Gordon, *op. cit.*, p. 595.

40 Sir George Sydenham Clarke, Governor of Victoria, in a speech titled 'The Navy and the Nation' delivered at a meeting of the Fitzroy branch of the Australian Natives Association, Fitzroy Town Hall, Melbourne, reported in *The Argus*, Thursday 11 June 1903 at http://trove.nla.gov.au/newspaper/article/9807954# (accessed on 10 June 2016).

INDEX